The Noble Quran

SELECTED PASSAGES FROM AL-QURAN AL-KAREEM WITH INTERPRETED MEANINGS

Dr. Muhammad Yunus Kumek

Medina House publishing

Cover Image: Marble Design, Courtesy of IOST Masjid,
Binghamton (Johnson City), New York
Interior background: Shutterstock.com

Medina Houseᶜ
publishing

www.medinahouse.org
170 Manhattan Ave,
PO Box 63
New York 14215
contact@medinahouse.org

Published in the United States of America.

BRIEF CONTENTS

Part 1

Introduction to Islam with Questions and Answers

Part 2

Selected Passages from Each Chapter of the Quran with Interpreted Meanings and Discussion Questions

Part 3

Appendix: Preferred Methodology of Translation of the Quran

CONTENTS

Part 3: Preferred Methodology of Translation of the Quran. . . 231

PART 1
INTRODUCTION TO ISLAM WITH
QUESTIONS AND ANSWERS

What is the Quran?

The Quran is the explanation of the universe. The Quran is the translator of the meanings of the different signs in one's personal and social life. The Quran is the translator of the meanings of the different signs in nature, the universe, and galaxies, in the known and unknown dimensions. The Quran is the explanation of the seen and unseen and mystical and literal realities. The Quran is the opener of the secrecies of Allah سبحانه وتعالى on the earth and in the skies. The Quran is the explanation of personal experiences and social encounters. The Quran is the language of the unseen world in the seen world of ours. The Quran is the reflection and explanation of the favors, Mercy and Caring of Allah سبحانه وتعالى on humans. The Quran is the pillar of Islam. The Quran is the map of the afterlife. The Quran is the explanation of the Names, and Attributes of Allah سبحانه وتعالى. The Quran is the teacher of the humans. The Quran is the water and food of Islam. The Quran is the essence of humanity. The Quran is the real guidance of humanity for peace. The Quran is a book of guidance, a book of prayer, a book of wisdom, a book of worship, a book of invitation, a book of chant, and a book of reflection and critical thinking. The Quran is the book of compilation of all other books that contain the essentials for the person's spiritual and emotional needs. The Quran is the source of all the branches of different paths followed by different prophets, messengers, saints and friends of Allah سبحانه وتعالى. The Quran is the Word of Allah سبحانه وتعالى. The Quran is the declaration of Allah سبحانه وتعالى, as the Creator of everything. The Quran is the address of Allah سبحانه وتعالى, who is the Creator of the earth, galaxies, universes, and skies. The Quran is the mutual conversation with the perspective of Rububiyah, upbringing, teaching and guidance of Allah سبحانه وتعالى. The Quran is the eternal sermon with the Perfect Authority of Allah سبحانه وتعالى. The Quran is the Favor of the Most Merciful due to the Divine Infinite Mercy. The Quran is a Divine Favor, Kindness, and Sympathy from the Creator to the creation. The Quran is the communication from the Most High and Exalted with some secret codes.

Therefore, the title of "the Word of Allah سبحانه وتعالى" has always and will always be given to the Quran.

The Quran is the final Book of Allah سبحانه وتعالى. Therefore, the Quran includes all the previous Books sent by Allah سبحانه وتعالى. Therefore, the Quran encompasses all the previous Books without any darkness of skepticism and doubts. The Quran is with certainty the revelation from Allah سبحانه وتعالى. The objective of the Quran is eternal happiness and peace. The inside of the Quran is guidance. The front of the Quran is the required light of belief. The back of the Quran is the proof with certainty. The right side of the Quran is the submission of the heart and conscience. The left side of the Quran is the acceptance and surrender of the mind, intellect, reason and logic. The fruit of the Quran is the mercy of Allah سبحانه وتعالى and happiness and peace in this world and afterlife. The Quran is the Divine Revelation signified and engaged by the angels, humans, jinns, animals, stones, clouds, mountains, animate, and inanimate beings.

The Quran inspires the person depending on the need of the person. The Quran opens itself to the person according to the need, time, place and context of the person. Therefore, it is not a classical book written in the past whose teachings are over and not valid today. Yet, the teachings of the Quran are always fresh, and valid. The Quran has always been an interactive sacred book. The Quran can reveal all different meanings if the person knows how to approach to the Quran with genuine need, humbleness, and with the intention of benefitting from the Noble Quran.

The Quran especially emphasizes four themes:[25]

1. Tawhìd: The correct and true belief, knowledge and practice to establish a relationship with Allah سبحانه وتعالى Who is One and Unique.
2. Nubuwwah: The correct and true knowledge and practice about the role and purpose of the messengers and the Prophets عليهم السلام sent by Allah سبحانه وتعالى.
3. Hashr: The correct and true knowledge and practice about the resurrection, afterlife and accountability after death.
4. Adalah and I'badah: The correct and true knowledge and practice about justice, ethics, morality and worship.

What is Islam?

According to Muslim faith, Islam is not a new religion but the continuation of the original message of Abraham عليهم السلام, Moses عليهم السلام, Jesus عليهم السلام, and other prophets and messengers of Allah سبحانه وتعالى. The creed, main message, of Islam is worshipping one and only Creator, Allah سبحانه وتعالى alone and not involving any associates with Allah سبحانه وتعالى implicitly or explicitly. In other words, Islam came to Muhammad (PBUH) in Arabia in 610 CE just to revive and reinstate the original message sent to Jesus عليهم السلام, Moses عليهم السلام, Abraham عليهم السلام, and other messengers.

Islam is the fastest growing and the second largest religion in the world. The number of its followers was approaching two billion in 2015. Islam is also the fastest growing religion in the United States and Europe.[1] We see and interact with Muslims in our daily lives and watch news every day related to them. There is an increasing demand in the job market, which would entail knowing Muslim culture.

Who is Allah?

The main tenet of Islam is the belief in <u>One Creator</u>. In Islam, Allah سبحانه وتعالى is the proper name of the Creator among many other names and attributes of Allah سبحانه وتعالى, but the same one and only Creator for Christianity and Judaism. There is no separate deity. Whether the Creator is referred to as God in English, or as YHWH in Hebrew, or as Allah سبحانه وتعالى in Arabic, it does not matter. The Creator is one. A person has a name to identify him or herself. The Creator may have different names, but the proper name of the Creator in Islam is "Allah سبحانه وتعالى." The word Allah سبحانه وتعالى has neither a plural form nor different gender nouns. Allah سبحانه وتعالى is not he, she, nor it. Because of the limitations of language, "He" is the pronoun used when referring to the noun "Allah سبحانه وتعالى" in English, although there is no humanly gender association. In the languages without gender pronouns, these pronouns are used to refer to Allah سبحانه وتعالى to minimize the issues due to anthropomorphism. Islamic scholars of philosophy[1] historically wrote

---

1. Science of kalam.

in various discourses the logical necessity of existence of the Creator, and the logical deduction of the oneness of Allah سبحانه وتعالى and perfection in Allah's سبحانه وتعالى attributes.[2]

Different Names (Attributes) of Allah سبحانه وتعالى

The Quran suggests that anyone can call Allah سبحانه وتعالى by any beautiful name,

> Say: "Call upon as Allah, or call upon as the Most Merciful: by whatever name you call, to Allah belongs the Most Beautiful Names . . . . " [17:110]

A few of the names or attributes of Allah سبحانه وتعالى mentioned in the Quran are: the All Merciful,[2] the Very Compassionate and Merciful,[3] the Knower of All,[4] and the Just.[5] Some of these names are presented on the following page.

In Islam, the different names and means of addressing the Creator are not as important as the recognition and realization of the presence of only one Creator. After the initial belief of Oneness and Uniqueness of the Creator, it is expected for one to learn and practice the beliefs, rituals, and humane dealings to ensure that the Creator will be pleased according to the Islamic teachings.

Whenever the name of Allah سبحانه وتعالى is recited or uttered, Muslims add the phrase of respect next to the proper name of the Creator. For example, Allah سبحانه وتعالى, Jalla Jalāluhu (JJ) which means the Most High, or Subhanahu Wa T'ăla (SWT) which means Allah سبحانه وتعالى is the Exalted One who is far from all deficiencies.

Muslims believe in one Creator. Allah سبحانه وتعالى is the same Creator who sent revelations at different times to different prophets and messengers, such as the *Torah* (Old Testament) to Moses عليهم السلام and *the Gospel* (injil) to Jesus عليهم السلام. In Islamic creed, creation

---

2. Ar-Rahman.
3. Ar-Rahem.
4. Al-Alim.
5. Al-Adl.

encompasses everyone—animals, trees, stones, skies, planets, stars, microscopic viruses, and everything other than the Creator. Allah سبحانه وتعالى is the Creator. Allah سبحانه وتعالى is One. Allah سبحانه وتعالى is Unique in the Divine Attributes. Allah سبحانه وتعالى does not resemble any of the creation. Allah سبحانه وتعالى does not have a father or a mother. Allah سبحانه وتعالى does not give birth. Allah سبحانه وتعالى does not need anything because need indicates dependence and that would be a defect for the Creator. On the other hand, all the creation, everything and everyone, needs Allah سبحانه وتعالى. The created can only understand Allah سبحانه وتعالى through the Divine Attributes. Allah's سبحانه وتعالى attributes are described in the Holy Quran and in the Hadith, the sayings of the Rasulullah ﷺ.

There are a lot of chapters and verses in the Quran that describe the attributes of Allah. One of the famous chapters is the chapter of Ikhlas (Sincerity).

Arabic to English Transliteration of the Chapter of Ikhlas (Sincerity):

Bismillah ir-Rahman ir-Raheem

1. Qul huwa Allahu Ahad
2. Allahu 's-Samad
3. Lam yalid wa lam yulad
4. Wa lam yakul lahu kufuwan Ahad

Various English Translations of the Verses of Chapter of Ikhlas (Sincerity):

1. English Translation by Muhammad Shameem, Mohammad Wali Raazi, and Muhammad Taqi Usmani[3]:

Say, "The truth is: Allah سبحانه وتعالى is One. Allah is Besought of all, needing none. [He neither begot anyone, nor was He begotten. And never has any one been equal to Him."]

2. English Translation by Mohammed Marmaduke Pickthall[4]:

Say: He is Allah سبحانه وتعالى, the One! [Allah سبحانه وتعالى, the eternally Besought of all! He begets not nor is he begotten. And there is none comparable unto Him.]

3.   English Translation by Yusuf Ali[5]:

Say: He is Allah سبحانه وتعالى, the One and Only; Allah, the Eternal, the Absolute; He begets not, nor is He begotten; And there is none comparable unto Him.

Simpler Translation and Explanation of the Chapter of Ikhlas (Sincerity):

Oh Muhammad صلى الله عليه وسلم! Proclaim that Allah سبحانه وتعالى is One. (Another verse which compels people to think that if there is more than one creator there will be chaos in the universe.)

Allah سبحانه وتعالى does not need anyone/anything, but everyone and everything needs Allah سبحانه وتعالى. (Need is a defect for the Creator.)

Allah سبحانه وتعالى does not give birth. Allah سبحانه وتعالى does not have a child or children. Allah سبحانه وتعالى does not have a father or a mother. (The Creator should not be dependent on a father or mother. Allah سبحانه وتعالى has no beginning and end according to the Islamic creed.)

There is nothing comparable to Allah سبحانه وتعالى.

Muslims recite this chapter all the time both during prayers as well as outside of prayers to get rewards from Allah. The reward for reading this short chapter is great because it explains the attributes of Allah.

On the other hand, it is forbidden to reflect on the essence and entity of the Creator. The creation is limited by the capacity of his mind, vision, hearing, and all other physical conditions. Therefore, the limited creation cannot grasp the Unlimited Creator. One of the established notions in Islamic creed is that understanding the Creator is gaining the understanding that the person cannot fully understand Allah سبحانه وتعالى, because the limited cannot understand the Unlimited. Understanding something means grasping or surrounding intellectually. Allah سبحانه وتعالى the Infinite cannot be, therefore, grasped with the limited creation. In the Quran, it says "The eyes cannot encompass Allah سبحانه وتعالى but Allah سبحانه وتعالى can encompass the eyes . . ." [6:103].

On the other hand, for many mystic Muslims the purpose of life is getting closer to Allah with worship and knowledge. This is not a physical closeness. Allah is closer to the person than him or herself but the person can be disconnected. This is sometimes referred to as knowledge of Allah سبحانه وتعالى.[6] In this perspective, the knowledge of the Creator is essential in Islamic theology. It is understood that "the Quran's heart is beating as the oneness of the Creator." Therefore, one of the main focuses in the Quran is the true understanding of Allah سبحانه وتعالى. Therefore, it is an orthodox teaching that any type of knowledge deprived of this will not be complete.

Who is Rasulullah ﷺ?

Muhammad is the name of the last prophet in Islam صلى الله عليه وسلم. He is a human role model, selected by Allah سبحانه وتعالى to confirm the previous messages of other role model messengers such as Jesus عليه السلام, Moses عليه السلام, and Abraham عليه السلام. The collective wisdom of humanity is constructed by the Prophets عليه السلام according to the Islamic scholars. There are only twenty-five names mentioned in the Quran about different prophets (PBUT). According to one narration from Rasulullah ﷺ, Allah سبحانه وتعالى sent more than 124,000 prophets at different times to different groups of people since the beginning of human history.[6] Because Allah سبحانه وتعالى is merciful and caring, Allah سبحانه وتعالى would not leave humans without any guidance and purpose on earth. Some scholars are also of the opinion that Buddha or Confucius could be prophets of Allah سبحانه وتعالى but people changed their original teachings over time.[7]

The Rasulullah ﷺ received prophethood at the age of forty. He had a very distinctive life before prophethood, compared to his fellows in his society. Some of his traits before prophethood were:

► He did not worship the idols, which was the main religion of his society.
► He recognized the One and Only Creator.

---

6. Ma'rufatullah in Arabic.

- He was known by his peers in his society with his ethical and virtuous traits.
- He was respected, and consulted in decision-making due to his trustworthiness.
- He was given responsibilities to protect valuables, orphans and women, due to his trustworthiness.
- He opposed certain practices of his society such as female infanticide, usury, and tribal wars due to blood vengeance.
- He performed spiritual retreats before his prophethood. In his spiritual retreats, he contemplated and was concerned about unethical practices of his society.

One can refer to other books[8][9] on the detailed traits and character of Rasulullah ﷺ. After receiving revelation from Allah سبحانه وتعالى at the age of forty, he became the messenger of Allah سبحانه وتعالى, living among the people and teaching the verses of the Quran as it was revealed to him, in his remaining life of twenty-three years. An example of a verse from the Quran that Rasulullah ﷺ is required to disclose what has been revealed to him is as follows [5:67]:

> O Messenger, announce that which has been revealed to you from your Sustaining, Nourishing, Nurturing Rabb, and if you do not, then you have not conveyed Allah's message. And Allah will protect you from the people. Indeed, Allah does not guide the people who are unappreciators and unrecognizers of Allah.

In other words, Rasulullah ﷺ is instructed not to hide even a little portion from the revelation. If this was not the case, then his true prophethood would have been challenged. In the above verse, Allah سبحانه وتعالى is giving assurance that the Prophet صلى الله عليه وسلم will be under the protection of Allah سبحانه وتعالى. After the revelation of the verse [5:67], the Prophet صلى الله عليه وسلم removed all types of escort systems of protectio,n although there were a lot of incidents to assassinate him, either through physical attack, poisoning, or black magic,[10][11] as mentioned in different sources of Islamic history and hadith. The words "hadith" or "sunnah" can refer to the statements and actions of Rasulullah ﷺ, as well as the conditions that were approved by him in his lifetime.

The humanness of Rasulullah ﷺ is frequently underlined and emphasized in Islam. Although Rasulullah ﷺ is the main teacher and messenger in Islam and venerated exceptionally, he is a creation, human, and worshipper of Allah سبحانه وتعالى. This notion itself is much emphasized in the Quran and in the sayings of Rasulullah ﷺ as well. The reason for this is to prevent any type of idolatry through disproportionate veneration except worshipping One God سبحانه وتعالى alone. According to the Islamic history, most of the idols were either prophets or saints of Allah سبحانه وتعالى in different times and had become idols due to disproportionate veneration.[12] Therefore, this teaching prevails repeatedly in the Islamic system of creed. In the Quran,

> Say [O Prophet]: I am but a mortal man like all of you. However, it has been revealed unto me that your God is the One and Only God. Hence, whoever looks forward [with hope and awe] to meeting his Sustainer [on Judgment Day], let him do righteous deeds, and let him not ascribe unto anyone or anything a share in the worship due to his Sustainer!" [18:110].[13]

> Say thou, [O Prophet:] "I am but a mortal like you. It has been revealed, to me that your God is the One God: go, then, straight towards to Allah and seek Allah's forgiveness!" And woe unto those who ascribe divinity to any other besides Allah [41:6].[13]

The upcoming section shows also the example of the miracles of Rasulullah ﷺ as the unordinary or unusual occurrences with the empowerment of Allah سبحانه وتعالى to prove his prophecy.

According to hadith scholars, it was a huge deal to preserve all the knowledge about the life of the Prophet صلى الله عليه وسلم in much detail for the upcoming generations. Therefore, one can find books narrated from the immediate companions of Rasulullah ﷺ, even about how long the eyelashes of the Prophet صلى الله عليه وسلم were, how many hairs the Prophet صلى الله عليه وسلم had, how his hand felt when one touched it, how his posture was when he was talking to the people, etc.[7]

What is the Quran?

The Quran is the name of the sacred text of Muslims. The Quran is a sacred book confirming and protecting the messages of the Bible: the Gospel, the Psalms, and the Torah.

The Quran was revealed to Rasulullah ﷺ in twenty-three years through the angel Gabriel عليه السلام. There are verses in the Quran that describes itself as the light and guidance for the one who wants to be guided and to transform her or himself from piles of spiritual darkness and oppression to light and freedom. There are passages in the Quran about how the Quran itself should be read and benefitted from. It strongly advises that it should be read with reflection and thinking.[7] While one is reading the Quran during and outside of prayers, it is the traditional practice of Rasulullah ﷺ and Muslims that they engage themselves with the text as an interactive interface. For example, when a person is reading the verses related to reward and Heaven, a person may ask Allah سبحانه وتعالى to be included with the people of Heaven. While reading the verses of punishment, a person may ask Allah's سبحانه وتعالى protection from it. When a person is reading the verses related to the applications of moral behavior, one can ask Allah سبحانه وتعالى about being just and ethical in one's positions of authority.[11]

According to the Quranic verses, the Quran was revealed by Allah سبحانه وتعالى not to oppose the Bible: the Gospel, the Psalms, and the Torah, but it came to confirm them. The second quality of the Quran is to protect the authenticity of the Bible: the Gospel, the Psalms, and the Torah. This is mentioned in the below verse of the Quran:

> Then We revealed the Book to you (O Muhammad!) with Truth, confirming whatever of the Book was revealed before, and protecting and guarding over it. [5:48]

There are numerous verses in the Quran referring to the Bible: the Gospel, the Psalms, and the Torah. In these verses of the Quran, Allah سبحانه وتعالى mentions the sameness of the message that was revealed

---

7. Tadabbur in Ar.

in all these sacred texts about worshipping only One God and not associating open or secret partnership with Allah سبحانه وتعالى.

The preparation for the afterlife, and the existence of rewards and punishment, are other important and frequent topics that are discussed in the Quran. The Quran critiques the dealings of the clergy of the previous books, such as the Bible: the Gospel, the Psalms, and the Torah, in their attempts to change the original teachings of the revelation from Allah سبحانه وتعالى. In numerous verses in the Quran, this is described as "selling the verses of Allah سبحانه وتعالى for a cheap worldly price." According to the Quran, one of the major examples of the alteration of the authenticity of the previous sacred texts is about the verses related to the correct understanding of Allah سبحانه وتعالى.

The Quran strongly condemns the defaming, offensive, and insulting narratives of other prophets and messengers in the Bible: the Gospel, the Psalms, and the Torah. These narratives are also considered to be the altered portions of the Bible: the Gospel, the Psalms, and the Torah, according to Islamic scholarship.[14]

Alternatively, one can find the narratives of the Virgin Mary عليها السلام, Moses عليه السلام, Abraham عليه السلام, Lot عليه السلام, and Jesus عليه السلام repetitively in the Quran with similar and different contextual meanings. One can notice a lot of similarities and differences with the Bible: the Gospel, the Psalms, and the Torah in certain perspectives. The differences of the prophetic narratives of the Quran compared to the narratives in the Bible: the Gospel, the Psalms, and the Torah are mostly about the ethical and pious stances of the prophets عليه السلام as role models.

On the other hand, in other instances, the Quran applauds the sincerity of some of the Christians who reflect on the verses of Allah سبحانه وتعالى in the universe, and take lessons from them in awe, respect, and fear. The Quran approves the ethical stance of Jews in different times supporting the good and preventing evil. In all cases of the narratives of the previous nations following Christianity and Judaism, they are presented as the true believers of their time. Their virtues and mistakes are mentioned in the Quran for readers in order to take a lesson from it but not to form isolating social and religious groups. Below is a piece from Carl Ernst's book of *How to read the Quran*:

> While the Quran overlaps with the Bible on certain subjects, it is unfamiliar enough in its distinctive narratives and in its stylistic peculiarities that many first-time readers have pronounced it to be impenetrable. The strangeness of the Quran for the Jewish and Christian reader lies in the fact that it does not repeat earlier biblical texts but instead makes brief allusions to them while providing a new and original synthesis that departs from familiar ways of reading the Old and New Testaments. (p. 4.)[15]

The Quran does not establish a mere group identity based on cultural inheritance of religion. Rather, it encompasses all the religions, especially Judaism, Christianity, and Islam, and critiques and constructs a pure, natural, but at the same time, logical way of belief and lifestyle for humanity. An unfamiliar reader of the Quran can be mistaken if the verses are taken out of their cultural, historical, and reason-based contexts. This problem can be true for any type of literal or out-of-context readings for any religious or non-religious books. Therefore, it is important to analyze the Quran as one whole piece in accordance with interpretations of Rasulullah ﷺ as found in the traditions or hadith.

There are different opinions about why the Quran is a miracle. It is a miracle because of its prophecies about scientific and social events. According to some, the Quran was revealed with a very unique style, especially when the Arab poetry and literature was at its zenith. There have been people who became Muslim after being exposed to the Quranic verses since the beginning of the revelation. Some contemporary scholars argue that the Quran never gets old, although human texts tend to lose their attraction over time. The Quran has always been compatible with scientific discoveries, and for the solutions of the social and individual problems according to Islamic scholars.[16] One of the interesting perspectives noted by the contemporary scholars[17] is that the Quran uses different languages in different instances. For example, when it is talking about a person's spiritual and evil problems, a physician's language is used instead of engineering language. The interpretation is that humans are complicated. It takes time to get sick and it takes time to heal. It is not like engineering where one can find the problem and fix it immediately. The cases of hypocrisy, denial, unappreciative behavior, self-conceit, arrogance, oppression, abuse, hate, and aggression are some of the diseases mentioned in the Quran. One can, for example, find the methodology of pathology in social diseases when observing the issues of moral philosophy.

Authenticity of the Quran

The Quran was revealed from Allah to Rasulullah ﷺ in Arabic in twenty-three years. As the verses were being revealed from Allah سبحانه وتعالى, the Prophet عليه السلام had special individuals[8] assigned for writing the revelation while the Prophet عليه السلام was alive. Besides this, as the revelation continued, the general public of the companions and friends[9] of Rasulullah ﷺ both memorized the verses and wrote them on different types of writing materials. The primary motivation of writing and memorization of the verses for the early Muslims was to recite the revealed verses in their own prayers. In a Muslim daily prayer,[10] a person should recite the Quranic verses from memory. This practice made thousands of followers memorize the entire Quran. Although writing and recording the Quran did exist during the time of the Prophet عليه السلام, one of the main ways of preserving the Quran has been through the tradition of memorization. In the education of this oral tradition, as the Islamic governments were established, it has become a tradition to open specialized memorization schools[11] of the Quran.[12] In this method of preservation of the Quran, Muslims have been meticulous even pronouncing one letter of the Quran correctly in its flawless recitation. This science is referred to as the correct recitation of the Quran, tajweed. For example, if a person attends a Muslim prayer in a mosque or in any place, it is better and rewarded more when everyone prays in congregation according to the teachings of the Prophet عليه السلام. To implement this teaching, a person stands

---

8. Referred to as the revelation writers.
9. Sahabah in Ar.
10. Referred to as Salah in Arabic speaking cultures and namaz in Indian, Persian, and Turkish cultures.
11. Sometimes called madrasa.
12. This is known as "Hifz" in Arabic. Hafiz is the honarary title given to the person who memorized the entire Quran.

in the front to lead the prayer.[13] This person loudly reads the Quranic verses from memory and the people behind listen to him. If this person makes a mistake in recitation of the Quran, then one can observe and hear that the followers are correcting the lead person. This tradition has been practiced since the beginning of Islam in both Arab and non-Arab cultures.

It is required to recite the Quran in Arabic because the Quran was revealed in the Arabic language. Any translation is considered as an interpretation although the meanings can be close. Therefore, one can find lengthy titles such as "the translation of the meaning of the Quran with interpretive meanings" in the translated versions of the Quran. The purpose is to simply tell the reader that what the person is reading is not the authentic and original Quran but approximated meanings in that language of translation. The original and authentic sacred text, the Quran, is in Arabic, not in any other language. This emphasis is also made in various verses of the Quran itself that the Quran is in Arabic, not in any other language.

This does not mean that a non-Arab should not read the Quran. It is encouraged to read the translations with explanatory notes to give the context and intended meanings rather than looking merely on the simple and possibly incorrect misleading literal meanings of the words in the translated language. This is true even for Arab readers as well because knowing the rules of the proper language and knowing the Quranic sciences needs separate training and education.

What do Muslims believe?

Six Faith Pillars of Islam

Iman is generally translated as the Islamic belief system. A person who has iman is called a believer (mu'min) in Islam. Islamic faith (iman) is based on six parts. These six parts include believing in

- ▶ The Creator (Allah)
- ▶ The Books

---

13. Referred to as Imam.

- ▶ The Prophets عليه السلام
- ▶ The Angels
- ▶ The Afterlife
- ▶ The Destiny

In Islamic terminology, belief is a dual process that requires believing from the heart as well as advocating that belief is through speech, that is, by speaking using the tongue. The tongue and the heart are, therefore, the two complimentary physical organs that satisfy the needs of Islamic faith.

Who is Allah سبحانه وتعالى؟

Belief in the Creator

In Islamic terminology, the explanation of the concept of the unity of Allah سبحانه وتعالى or the Creator is referred to as tawhid. Tawhid might be translated as Islamic monotheism. The opposite of tawhid is shirk, which could be referred to as polytheism. In Islam, the branch of the science that explains tawhid is called kalam or aqaid. One of the famous scholars of this science is Imam Tahawi. He explains the core principles of tawhid very concisely in his book called *Aqidah Tahawiyah*.[18] Below is my rendering of a partial translation from his work.

Allah سبحانه وتعالى: The Divine and the Creator

Allah سبحانه وتعالى is One, without any partners. There is nothing like Allah سبحانه وتعالى. There is nothing that can overwhelm Allah سبحانه وتعالى. There is no god other than Allah سبحانه وتعالى. Allah سبحانه وتعالى is the Eternal without a beginning and enduring without end. Allah سبحانه وتعالى will never perish nor come to an end. No imagination can conceive of Allah سبحانه وتعالى and no understanding can comprehend Allah سبحانه وتعالى. Allah سبحانه وتعالى is different from any created being. Allah سبحانه وتعالى is living and never dies and is eternally active and never sleeps. Allah سبحانه وتعالى creates without being in need to do so and provides for the creation without any effort. Allah سبحانه وتعالى causes death with no fear and restores to life without difficulty. Allah

سبحانه وتعالى has always existed together with the eternal attributes since before creation. Bringing creation into existence did not add anything to Allah's سبحانه وتعالى attributes that were not already there. As Allah سبحانه وتعالى was, together with the attributes, in pre-eternity, so Allah سبحانه وتعالى will remain throughout endless time. It was not only after the act of creation that Allah سبحانه وتعالى could be described as "the Creator," nor was it only by the act of origination that Allah سبحانه وتعالى could be described as "the Originator."

Allah سبحانه وتعالى was always the Lord even when there was nothing to be Lord of, and always the Creator even when there was no creation. Allah سبحانه وتعالى is exalted beyond having opposites or equals. Anyone who describes Allah سبحانه وتعالى as being in any way the same as a human is not a believer. All those who grasp this will take heed and refrain from saying things such as the unbelievers say, and they will know that Allah سبحانه وتعالى, in the attributes, is not like human beings. Allah سبحانه وتعالى is beyond having limits placed on Allah سبحانه وتعالى, or being restricted, or having parts or limbs. Nor is Allah سبحانه وتعالى contained by the six directions as all created things are. Allah سبحانه وتعالى encompasses all things and what Allah سبحانه وتعالى has created is incapable of encompassing Allah سبحانه وتعالى. Allah سبحانه وتعالى has absolute control over everything and nothing has any control over Allah سبحانه وتعالى. Nothing can be independent of Allah سبحانه وتعالى even for the blinking of an eye, and whoever considers herself or himself independent of Allah سبحانه وتعالى for the blinking of an eye is guilty of unbelief.[18]

Why is belief in one god the core of Islam?

Three of the major sins in Islam are not believing in one Creator, transgressing the rights of parents, and killing someone as narrated by the Prophet عليه السلام.[19] According to some scholars, these three cases are all related. A child who does not recognize and appreciate the right of a mother and father is considered in the state of a major denial of the favors of the parents. These favors could be a mother going through hardship of carrying her child for nine months in the state of sickness and pains of labor and delivery, breastfeeding after birth, and physical and spiritual upbringing of the child by both mother and the father. This unappreciative state of the child could be due to arrogance or denial, despite being aware of all these favors. In a similar way, according to Islamic creed, Allah gives a very minute role to the parents about upbringing a child compared to the Divine role but expects an immense appreciation to the favors of the parents. By doing this, this may lead a person either to go to Heaven or it may harshly cause the person to go for a just accountability. In other words, according to Islam, Allah سبحانه وتعالى deserves more appreciation and recognition about the Divine favors than parents. In reality, Allah سبحانه وتعالى is the one who gives life in a mother's womb, giving sustenance, strength, and all the ecological and social environment for a person to exist. The Divine expectation is that the person knows, accepts, and appreciates that there is a Creator who has given all these bounties to the person. The person appreciates it firstly by believing in the One and only Creator, then he or she could be called in a state of appreciation called a believer or a Muslim. Then, as a believer, finding ways to please Allah سبحانه وتعالى through the ways of the Prophets عليه السلام such as Muhammad صلى الله عليه وسلم who represents in his prophetic teachings the paths of the previous messengers, and prophets such as Jesus عليه السلام, Moses عليه السلام, David عليه السلام, Abraham عليه السلام, and so forth. The roles of the Prophets عليه السلام are all complimentary to each other and they are not in the state of competing and conflicting with each other.

How do Muslims understand miracles?

Miracles

In Islamic belief, prophets and messengers of Allah سبحانه وتعالى are empowered to show miracles to prove that their message is the truth. In other words, the main purpose of a miracle is to prove the truthfulness and sincerity of the apostle. Showing miracles is only one vehicle for the authenticity of the true messengership or prophethood. Miracles[14] occur

---

14. Mu'jizah in Ar.

only with the help of Allah's وتعالى سبحانه power[15] and knowledge.[16] If any prophet or messenger or apostle performs a miracle, it is the Creator (Allah وتعالى سبحانه) who gives them that empowerment to do so.

The Quran mentions several miracles in relation to the Prophets عليه السلام Abraham السلام عليه, Moses السلام عليه, Jesus السلام عليه, and many others. The Quran mentions, for example, the miracle of fire not burning Abraham السلام عليه, the burning bush encounter of Moses السلام عليه, and the birth of Jesus السلام عليه without any father from Virgin Mary عليه السلام.

According to the Islamic doctrine, the supreme miracle of the Rasulullah ﷺ is the Quran itself because it is still unchanged, authentic, and it is still alive with people. The Quran has in itself convoluted miracles, miracles within miracles, related to prophecies, scientific discoveries, therapeutic effects, language, literature, rationality, and philosophy according to many exegetical scholars.[16] This scripture, the Quran, was revealed to a person, Muhammad وسلم عليه الله صلى, who was not a sophisticated or a complex intellectual or a philosopher rather an unsophisticated, pure, innocent, genuine and sincere person known in his society to be the model of his ethical norms prior to Islam. Although Rasulullah ﷺ performed various miracles such as curing the sick, stones talking with him, and trees witnessing his sacred messengership from Allah سبحانه وتعالى, splitting the moon, gushing water coming from his fingers at the time of draught and thousands of people quenching their thirst with this water, yet his remaining legacy as a miracle is considered to be the Quran and this miracle is still with people as mentioned unanimously by Islamic scholars.[20]

Who is a prophet or messenger in Islam?

Believing in Prophets

Muslims are required to believe in all true messengers and prophets of Allah وتعالى سبحانه sent in different times with a mission by Allah سبحانه

---

15. Qudrah in Ar.
16. I'lm in Ar.

وتعالى. In Islam, it is required to believe in Jesus عليه السلام, Moses عليه السلام, Abraham عليه السلام, and all others sent by Allah سبحانه وتعالى. Therefore, if a Muslim makes a statement that "I believe in Muhammad صلى الله عليه وسلم but I don't believe in Jesus عليه السلام," then according to the canonized Islamic creed system, this person is not a Muslim.[18]

The understanding of prophets or messengers sent by Allah سبحانه وتعالى is somehow similar and different than the Judeo-Christian tradition. In Islamic narratives and understanding, the Prophets عليه السلام have certain attributes. They are role models, truthful, trusted, insightful, and infallible.[21] Infallibility is not because they are like angels. They have the choice and free will of doing evil or good but they always choose to do good and moral with mercy and protection of Allah سبحانه وتعالى. In other words, they use their free will in decision-making with their best implementation of decisions correctly and ethically. Therefore, one can find the Quranic and Biblical narratives about a messenger and a prophet of Allah سبحانه وتعالى being similar up to a point, then they diverge. The primary divergence point is the content of the Quranic narratives due to the infallibility and truthfulness of these messengers. According to different discourses,[22] it is not logical that Allah سبحانه وتعالى would send them as human examples but they would do otherwise. Therefore, the Prophets عليه السلام in Islam are sent by Allah سبحانه وتعالى as the role models to show that Allah's سبحانه وتعالى commands are practical and possible to implement as humans. One of the attributes of the Prophets and messengers of Allah عليه السلام سبحانه وتعالى is that they call people to the ethical, moral, and true recognition appreciation of One Creator. One can find very similar stories in such narratives as those about Abraham عليه السلام, Jonah عليه السلام, Noah عليه السلام, and Moses عليه السلام in the Quran, the Bible: the Gospel, the Psalms, and the Torah. One can even find similarities in the names of different prophets, messengers, and important people in Islam and Judeo-Christian tradition which may be surprising for the unfamiliar reader as some presented on the next page.

Name in Judeo-Christian Tradition	Name in Islam
Abraham	Ibrahim
Moses	Musa
David	Dawud
Solomon	Sulayman
Zechariah	Zakariya
Jesus	Isa
Noah	Nuh

It is interesting to note that Muslims refer to Jesus (PBUH) as "Jesus Christ." In other words, Muslims are required to believe in Jesus (PBUH) as the Christ due to teachings of the Quran and the Rasulullah ﷺ. Similarly, Muslims view John the Baptist (PBUH) the same as Christians. In other words, Muslims are required to believe that John was baptized due to the teachings of the Quran and Rasulullah ﷺ. The Arabic name for Virgin Mary (PBUH) is Maryam, the mother of Jesus (PBUH).

Muslims believe that Allah created all the community of beings with a purpose, with a guide or a leader. Allah gave bees a queen, ants a leader, and birds and fish each a guide, and a prophet for human beings to guide them to a spiritual, intellectual, and material perfection. Although it may be possible for some people to find the Creator by reflecting upon nature, but human beings still need a prophet or a messenger from Allah سبحانه وتعالى to learn why they were created, where they came from, where they are going, and how to worship the Creator properly. Allah سبحانه وتعالى sent prophets to teach the people the true meaning of creation, to unveil the mysteries behind historical and natural events, and to inform them of their relationship with the Divine Scriptures and the universe according to Islam.

Without prophets, human beings could not have made any scientific progress according to some Muslim scholars.[7] Prophets guided humanity in intellectual—and therefore scientific—illumination. Prophet Adam (PBUH) in farming, Prophet Enoch (PBUH) in tailoring,

Prophet Noah (PBUH) in ship making, and Joseph (PBUH) in clock making. Prophets have taught the guidelines of social life based on justice, respect, and ethical values.

Whenever people departed from the original teachings of a prophet, Allah سبحانه وتعالى sent another one to teach them again in both belief and ethical values. This continued until the coming of the last messenger ﷺ as mentioned in the Quran [33:40]. The prophethood and messengership ended with him although Allah sent different scholars and saints to revive the religion after the messenger ﷺ according to Islamic theology.

Muslims believe in all of the prophets and messengers (PBUT) and make no distinction among them as the verse in the Quran says (my contextual and exegetical translation):

> The prophet (PBUH) believed in the Revelation
> The believers believed in the Revelation
> Everyone believed in the One, and Only Allah سبحانه وتعالى
> Everyone believed in Gabriel (PBUH), Michael (PBUH), and
>   all angels
> Everyone believed in the Bible: the Gospel, the Psalms, and the
>   Torah, and Quran and all the scriptures
> Everyone believed in Moses (PBUH), Jesus (PBUH), and
>   Muhammad (PBUH) as the chosen messengers from Allah
>   سبحانه وتعالى
> Everyone believed the other messengers and all the prophets
>   (PBUT) chosen by Allah سبحانه وتعالى
> There is no superiority of one book over another
> There is no superiority of one prophet over another
> And they ended their proclamation as:
> We received the message and surrendered and submitted Oh
>   Allah سبحانه وتعالى.
> You are Our Please forgive us, our Nourishing, Sustaining Rabb
>   سبحانه وتعالى.
> We will meet with You soon [2:285]

The above verse is an example of why Muslims believe that Islam is a universal and inclusive religion.

Miracles and Divinity

In Islamic belief, the miracle of a prophet is similar to an ID card that Allah سبحانه وتعالى possibly sent this person, and this person is special. Showing a miracle is not a sufficient tool to be a prophet of Allah سبحانه وتعالى, but a possibility. Therefore, Allah سبحانه وتعالى empowers each prophet to show the miracles to their people to prove that this messenger's message is true. The main purpose of a miracle is to prove the truthfulness and sincerity of the apostle. Miracles occur only with the help of Allah's سبحانه وتعالى power and knowledge. If any prophet or messenger or apostle shows a miracle, it is the Creator (Allah سبحانه وتعالى) giving that empowerment. As mentioned in the Quran, Allah سبحانه وتعالى previously empowered the prophets (PBUH) and messengers such as Abraham (PBUH), Moses (PBUH), Jesus (PBUH), and many others. The Quran does not overtly describe the Prophet's (PBUH) various miracles. According to Islamic doctrine, the supreme miracle of Rasulullah ﷺ is the Quran itself because:

▶ The Quran was revealed to an illiterate person, Rasulullah ﷺ.
▶ The Quran talks about unseen and gives detailed information, such as stories of the past prophets and information about the future, such as the war between Byzantines and Persians.
▶ There are no contradictions in the Quran.
▶ It gives authentic information about nature and creation.
▶ The Quran contains information about society and relations between different groups.
▶ No verse of the Quran contradicts with scientific advancements.

Some of the other miracles of Rasulullah ﷺ are:

▶ The Prophet's (PBUH) exemplary moral and ethical life. Until the age of 40, before Prophethood, he was already an established role model in his community with his exemplary moral and ethical life.
▶ The earlier scriptures such as the Bible: the Gospel, the Psalms, and the Torah, forecasting about the upcoming of the Prophet ﷺ. The Christian and Jewish scholars were already in prediction from their scriptures about a new messenger of Allah سبحانه وتعالى coming in that region around the time of the Muhammad (PBUH).

▶ Splitting the moon. When the Prophet (PBUH) was challenged about the authenticity of his messengership from Allah سبحانه وتعالى, Rasulullah ﷺ split the moon by pointing to it with his finger as a miracle and kept it split in the range of seconds to minutes and then brought it back to its original form with the empowerment and enablement of Allah سبحانه وتعالى. This incident was narrated by numerous witnesses in the science of authentication of hadith.

▶ Heavenly journey-ascension. Rasulullah ﷺ ascended into the Heavens with the guide of the Arc Angel Gabriel (PBUH). On this heavenly journey, Rasulullah ﷺ met with all the prior messengers, such as Adam (PBUH), Noah (PBUH), Abraham (PBUH), Moses (PBUH) and Jesus (PBUH). They all prayed together in the leadership of Rasulullah ﷺ in Jerusalem. Finally, Rasulullah ﷺ met with Allah سبحانه وتعالى and Allah سبحانه وتعالى bestowed him with the five daily prayers as a gift for all the Muslims. Then, the Prophet (PBUH) came back to earth to complete his mission among people as the messenger of Allah سبحانه وتعالى until his demise.

▶ Stones speaking in his hand. When Rasulullah ﷺ picked up a handful of stones from the ground, the pebbles started glorifying Allah سبحانه وتعالى as a miracle. This was witnessed by people next to him and they heard the chanting of the stones while the Prophet (PBUH) was holding them, according to the authentic chain of narrations.

▶ Poisoned meat telling him that it was poisonous, and that he should not eat it. Rasulullah ﷺ, with his companions were invited to dinner by a woman of prior scriptures. The woman put poison in the food to test if he was a real messenger of Allah سبحانه وتعالى. As a miracle, the cooked meat informed the Prophet (PBUH) that there was poison in it.

▶ Feeding hundreds of people with one bowl of food. It is reported that during a time of scarcity of food, the Prophet (PBUH) prayed on a bowl of food and then, hundreds of people ate from this bowl without the food finishing in the bowl.

▶ The loud cry of a wood pillar that the Prophet (PBUH) used to lean against in the mosque because it was being removed from the mosque and it was sad that it would not be able to see the Prophet (PBUH) again.

▶ Some of the animals talking to the Prophet (PBUH), and complaining of their abuse by their owners.

For all the incidents above, there are multiple authentic narrators and witnesses according to the Islamic tradition.[10]

In Islamic creed, the messengers perform supernatural events or miracles with the empowerment of the Creator, not through their own ability. Therefore, the full credit is given to the Creator. The Creator is divine and not the messenger or the Prophet (PBUH). Claiming divinity for any of Allah's سبحانه وتعالى creations including the prophets (PBUH) is an immense sin in Islam. Therefore, Muslims believe that Jesus (PBUH) is one of the selected apostles of the Creator along with other prophets such as Abraham (PBUH), Moses (PBUH), David (PBUH), Muhammad (PBUH), and others. No one is divine except Allah. The Quran explains that the creation of Jesus (PBUH) is similar to Adam (PBUH). Adam (PBUH) did not have a father and mother, as Jesus (PBUH) did not have a father as a miracle by the Creator. The below verses allude to this notion:

> The similitude of Jesus (PBUH) before Allah is as that of Adam;
> Allah created him from dust, then said to him "Be": and he was.
> [5] [the Quran, 3:59]

> O People of the Book! Commit no excesses in your religion: Nor say of Allah aught but the truth. Jesus Christ, the son of Mary was (no more than) a Messenger of Allah, and Allah's Word, which Allah bestowed on Mary, a Spirit proceeding from Allah, so believe in Allah and Allah's Messengers. Say not "Trinity", desist! it will be better for you. Your Creator, is indeed One Creator, Glory be to Allah, far Exalted is Allah above having a son. To Allah belong all things in the heavens and on earth. And, enough is Allah as a Disposer of affairs. [the Quran, 4:171]
> [5]

In another chapter in the Quran, there is a dialogue between Jesus (PBUH) and Allah:

> And behold! Allah will say: "O Jesus, the son of Mary! Did you say to human beings, 'Worship me and my mother as gods in derogation of Allah'?" He will say: "Glory to You! Never could I say what I had no right (to say). Had I said such a thing, though, you would indeed have known it. You know what is in my heart, although, I do not know what is in You. You know in full all that is hidden. [the Quran 5:116][5]

Muslim scholars interpret the above verses of the Quran as the clear indication of acceptance and declaration of Jesus (PBUH) that he is the created being of Allah, and Jesus (PBUH) was sent similar to other prophets to guide people to the teachings of Allah سبحانه وتعالى. So, Muslims believe that Jesus (PBUH) is an important prophet and messenger of Allah سبحانه وتعالى but not the son of Allah سبحانه وتعالى.

Do the Muslims believe in the Bible: the Gospel, the Psalms, and the Torah?

The Belief in the Books

Muslims are required to believe in all the books that were revealed by Allah سبحانه وتعالى. In the creed system, a Muslim is required to believe in the Quran, the Bible: the Gospel, the Psalms, and the Torah and all other communications sent by Allah سبحانه وتعالى. Therefore, if a person says "I believe in the Quran but I don't believe in the Bible: the Gospel, the Psalms, and the Torah that was sent by Allah سبحانه وتعالى," then this person is not a Muslim according to the canonized teachings.[18]

Muslims make a distinction that they believe in the authentic versions of these sacred books. Some of these books are mentioned in the Quran. They are the the Gospel (injil), the Psalms (zabur) and the torah (tawrah), and other books or pages that were revealed to different prophets at different times such as Adam (PBUH) and Abraham (PBUH). The Quran mentions that in all the previous books, Allah سبحانه وتعالى has stated the same message of worshipping one and only Allah سبحانه وتعالى. There is no change in the message but Allah سبحانه وتعالى sent at different times the same message due to the modification of the original message by the people over time as mentioned in the verses in the Quran:

> And when Allah took a promise from those who were given the earlier scriptures stating that "you must make it clear and explain this scripture to the people but not conceal it." But still they hid it and exchanged it for a cheap price. And what a bad and lowly deal that they did! [3:187]

> Oh followers of the earlier scriptures! there has come to you Our Messenger, Muhammad (PBUH) making clear to you much of what you used to conceal from the scriptures and overlooking much. There has come to you from Allah a light and a clear Book, the Quran. [5:15] (adapted from[23]).

Confirming Scripture or Confirming Book is another name the Quran uses for the divine revelation for itself. It is due to the understanding of the Quran as the scripture confirming the Christian Bible: the Gospel, the Psalms, and the Torah. The Quran values Christian, Jewish, and all other divine scriptures as the scriptures of Allah سبحانه وتعالى.

As stated[24]:

> The notion of the Confirming Book is one of the emphasizing notions in the theology of practice as well. In the accepted and canonized understanding of the scripture in the theology, the position of the Quran is not to compete with the Bible: the Gospel, the Psalms, and the Torah, but its position is to detail, confirm and complement the other divine books.[17] As an example: a genuine parent will not have preference among their children. He or she will expect the siblings to help each other. Similarly, the divine books in their essence stabilize each other in reaching one goal: achieving and establishing a path to the Divine.

---

17. Musaddiq is used in the Quran.

Are the angels in Islam similar to Christianity and Judaism?

Belief in Angels

Although there are rational arguments by Islamic scholars about the existence of angels, it is ultimately a belief that Muslims need to submit and accept that there are unseen beings other than humans that are created by Allah سبحانه وتعالى. In this case, these are angels who are created by Allah سبحانه وتعالى. They perform actions in the physical, metaphysical, seen, and unseen worlds with the order of Allah سبحانه وتعالى. There are angels who are with each person protecting them. There are angels who record the deeds of each person. One can realize the similar beliefs in the teachings of Christianity and Judaism with Islam. Therefore, one can even find similarities among these traditions for the specific names of angels. For example:

Name of the Angel in Judeo-Christian Tradition	Name of the Angel in Islam	Angel's Duty
Gabriel	Jabrael or Jibril	Bringing revelation from Allah سبحانه وتعالى to the selected messengers and prophets
Michael	Mikaeel	Maintaining the natural laws

One of the titles of Gabriel (PBUH) is Ruhul Qudus according to the exegetical scholars as mentioned in the Quran. This expression can translate as holy spirit into English. Therefore, some of the Muslim scholars explain the possible confusion of Christians in the interpretation of angel Gabriel (PBUH) as the part of the divinity, because this angel was bringing a message from Allah سبحانه وتعالى to the prophets (PBUH).

What is going to happen after death according to Islam?

Life after Death

Death is the movement of the soul from one place to another in Islam. Death is not an annihilation or an extinction. The theme of death is frequent as a reality in the Quran, in the sayings of the Rasulullah ﷺ, and in other books of the religion. Belief in the life after death is one of the main beliefs of Islam. The soul does not die but the body dies. The death is the meeting day of the opening of the unseen world.

After death in Islam symbolizes accountability. Everyone's life is based on accountability. A person has a free will but is accountable for their choices. Although there are similarities between Islam and other Judeo-Christian traditions in the belief of afterlife, the day of Judgment, Heaven and punishment, there are also some important differences.

The teachings of the Quran are very much based on the rational persuasion of the reader on the need of the recreation by Allah سبحانه وتعالى and accountability after death. In other words, the Quran expects not only the reader should believe but also should have the certainty of the faith in the afterlife and meeting with Allah سبحانه وتعالى.[24]

The understanding in the attributes of Allah سبحانه وتعالى also affects the understanding of the afterlife. In Islam, Allah سبحانه وتعالى is just and merciful. A person will face accountability in afterlife due to the attribute of Allah سبحانه وتعالى, the Just. At the same time, Allah سبحانه وتعالى is merciful. If a person expects forgiveness, Allah سبحانه وتعالى can still forgive this person as being the merciful. Therefore, in Islamic creed, there is the uncertainty of not knowing one's place in afterlife. Uncertainty forms a positive constant struggle in bettering oneself in the ethical norms and piety until one dies. This internal struggle can be called jihad. The attitude of uncertainty can lead the person to have a piety and virtue, not being arrogant but humble. The sinner can be hopeful because ultimately the mercy of Allah سبحانه وتعالى saves the person. Alternatively, the just attribute of Allah سبحانه وتعالى makes the person work hard in piety and have ethical behavior in order to deserve a good compensation of the lifelong struggle from Allah سبحانه وتعالى.

At the same time, the just attribute of Allah سبحانه وتعالى can stop and prevent an evil-doer or planner if this person knows that soon he or she will be accountable for self-induced actions.[25]

According to the narration from the Prophet (PBUH), no one will enter to Heaven with their deed they deserve but only with the mercy of Allah سبحانه وتعالى.[10] Although there is the constant motivation of doing good and avoiding evil with the reward and punishment system, it ultimately should not be the claim of the person with implicit and explicit arrogance that it is the right of this person to be in Heaven.

According to Islamic philosophy, a life after death is required with true and correct understanding of the deity. A merciful Allah سبحانه وتعالى does not create a sophisticated system, like the universe, and a sophisticated system like a human for only the average span of a human life of seventy years. The innate desire for a human not to die and to be eternal is itself a proof that there should be another place like afterlife. In Islamic intellectual reasoning, the practical necessities of afterlife are many as well. A person cannot console a small child when her mother dies. The only possible way to minimize her pain is to tell her that there is a place that she will meet her mother soon, like Heaven. An aging person, when all his or her loved ones are dying and this person is getting close to death day by day will be in torture unless he or she certainly believes that there is no extinction but an afterlife after death. A family life will not be on true grounds unless the long shared companionship does not end with death but the couples know that there is a life after death that they can be together.[25]

How is the understanding of evil, good, and destiny?

Destiny, Evil, and Good

According to the Islamic Creed, Allah سبحانه وتعالى knows everything past and future in one's life. But the person has a free will to choose the good or bad. Allah's سبحانه وتعالى knowledge of the future and events does not mean that Allah سبحانه وتعالى forces people to do their actions. Everyone is ultimately responsible for their actions. Through worship, repentance, and humbleness, a believer can regularly ask from Allah سبحانه وتعالى to always make the right choice, to do good, and for protection from the evil. For sure, Allah سبحانه وتعالى can answer the person's prayers and Allah سبحانه وتعالى is always hearing and active according to the Islamic theology.

However, it is expected for a person to embrace the trials, tests, and evil-looking incidents in order to acquire spiritual strength and increase one's spiritual ranks. At the same time, one should constantly ask for an easy and nice life with appreciation and gratitude of Allah سبحانه وتعالى. Nonetheless, how one responds to an evil is important to learn and actualize in religious and spiritual life. This response should be in a non-complaining mode but still show continuous appreciation and gratitude to Allah سبحانه وتعالى. Indeed, with greater rewards come greater trials. Indeed, when Allah سبحانه وتعالى loves a group of people, then Allah سبحانه وتعالى would test them. During these trials, when the person continues their duties with Allah سبحانه وتعالى with appreciation, gratitude, worship and prayer, then this person will be pleased and satisfied, and whoever is displeased, then they will have indignation.[26]

What are the worship requirements in Islam?

Five Worship Pillars of Islam

There are five required pillars of Islam. These are verbal declaration of the oneness of the Creator,[18] daily prayers,[19] fasting,[20] charity,[21] and pilgrimage.[22] All these pillars require the condition of a person being not insane, mentally sound, and being in the age of required maturity, approximately the age of puberty, fifteen years old.

---

18. Shahadah.
19. Salah in Arabic and namaz in Indian, Persian, and Turkish cultures.
20. Sawm in Arabic.
21. Zakah in Ar.
22. Hajj in Ar.

Who is considered a Muslim?

Declaration of Faith

The verbal declaration of oneness of the Creator is the creed of Islam. A Muslim is expected to admit that there is one Creator. Saying this in a statement verbally is required as a creed. This statement is "There is no deity but Allah سبحانه وتعالى." In Arabic, this statement is "La ilaha illa Allah." Once a person says this and believes this by heart this person is considered a Muslim. A person's recognition of the Rasulullah ﷺ as the messenger of Allah سبحانه وتعالى is required as well. The full expression of the declaration of faith is: There is no deity except Allah سبحانه وتعالى and Muhammad (PBUH) is messenger and prophet of Allah سبحانه وتعالى. In other words, recognizing all the messengers and prophets of Allah سبحانه وتعالى appear clearly by recognition of the Rasulullah ﷺ. With this, the full version of the declaration of faith can be: "I believe that there is no deity except only one Creator. I believe in the true message of Muhammad (PBUH) along with other prophets and messengers, Jesus (PBUH), Moses (PBUH), Abraham (PBUH), and others. I believe in all the original and authentic messages of the Quran, the Bible: the Gospel, the Psalms, and the Torah, and all the books sent truly by Allah سبحانه وتعالى. I believe in all the unseen and future events as told by Allah سبحانه وتعالى: the Angels, life after death, and the destiny."

This person will not be a true Muslim if he has some problems embodying this core concept of Islam. There is no requirement of public announcement of this declaration. This is between the person and Allah سبحانه وتعالى, though some of the contemporary scholars encourage new Muslims to declare it openly and publicly to form a social community support group. Although it is not required, there is a social encouragement to change the names of the new Muslims in the West to form a social and group identity within the immigrant Muslims who mostly have Arabic names. This practice is lately criticized by some of the emerging progressive Muslims that changing the name of the person is not required and was not practiced by the Prophet (PBUH) unless the name of the person had a bad meaning and the Prophet (PBUH) advised it to be changed in some occasions.[10]

What are the five daily prayers in Islam?

Five Times Daily Prayer

Muslims are required to pray five times daily. Each prayer is a different unit.[23] A unit includes three physical movements and reading of the Quranic verses and supplications:

1. Standing Position
2. Bowing Position
3. Prostration

Different positions in daily prayers

© zainabsoly/Shutterstock.com

---

23. Unit is rakah in Arabic.

For each prayer, there is a time interval that a Muslim is expected to pray. These are:

1. Morning Prayer:[24] It starts approximately an hour and a half before sunrise, with the real dawn and ends with sunrise.
2. Noon Prayer:[25] It starts approximately an hour after noon when the sun starts declining from the zenith position and lasts approximately three hours. The prayer interval continues until the start of the next prayer, which is the afternoon prayer.
3. Afternoon Prayer:[26] It starts at the end of noon prayer and ends with sunset. The prayer interval continues until the start of the next prayer, which is the sunset prayer.
4. Sunset Prayer:[27] It starts with sunset and ends after approximately an hour and a half. It continues until the start of the next prayer, which is the night prayer.
5. Night Prayer:[28] It starts at the end of the sunset prayer, where the sky loses totally its reddish color due to sunset. It continues until the start of the next prayer, which is the morning prayer.

Prayer	Start	End
Morning	5:23 am	6:41 am
Noon	1:00 pm	4:35 pm
Afternoon	4:35 pm	7:20 pm
Sunset	7:20 pm	8:38 pm
Night	8:38 pm	5:23 am

Above is an example of prayer times as a daily planner in Manhattan, New York, on April 1, 2018. Muslims find these set times of spiritual charge and discharge very valuable although it can be a few minutes.[24] The times of the daily prayer change depending on the location and time of the year. Five daily prayers are very crucial in a Muslim's life. Some of the scholars interpret from the saying of the Prophet (PBUH) that a person can have a sound, beneficial, and peaceful belief in Allah سبحانه وتعالى as long as she or he is careful not to miss five daily prayers.

---

24. Fajr prayer.
25. Zuhr Pr.
26. Asr Pr.
27. Magrib Pr.
28. Isha Pr.

It is required to pray at the time intervals for each prayer. If a person misses a prayer, then it is required for that person to make it up. Each prayer can take up to three to five minutes on average when the minimum conditions of a prayer are fulfilled. If the person cannot bow or go on the ground due to physical limitation, he or she can pray sitting or in other postures that are comfortable for this person.

What is fasting or Ramadan?

Fasting

Muslims are required to fast once a year for a full month. This month in Arabic is called Ramadan. Muslims follow the lunar calendar; therefore, Ramadan changes each year. During fasting, Muslims are not allowed to eat, drink, or have any sexual relationship from sunrise to sunset. After sunset, all the prohibitions are lifted till sunrise. A person can be excused not to fast due to sickness, old age, or traveling. In this case, this person is suggested to feed a person daily for each day that he or she missed fasting. The nights of the month of Ramadan are spiritually powerful. Therefore, it was the practice of the Rasulullah ﷺ to pray after breaking the fast[29] and enjoy it in long prayers. To encourage this practice, Muslims get together in Ramadan and pray on every night of this month and recite the Quran abundantly.

Are the Muslims required to give charity?

Charity

Muslims are required to give 2.5% of their excess money to the people who are in need. The excess money is the amount after one fulfills his or her basic needs of food, house, and transportation. After these needs, if he or she has an excess then 2.5% of this should be given to the poor every year. If the person does not have any excess money after the basic needs of food, home, and transportation expenses then there is no requirement of charity on this person.

---

29. This prayer is called tarawih in Arabic.

What is Muslim's pilgrimage or Hajj?

Pilgrimage

A Muslim is required to visit the holy sites once in his or her lifetime. This requirement exists if the person has the financial means to travel and support his or her family during his or her absence. If the person does not have enough financial means, then this person is not required to perform a pilgrimage. Another condition for this requirement is the permissibility of the person's health conditions for travel.

The Kabah

The Kabah is a small cubicle building located in the city of Makkah in Saudi Arabia. Muslims believe that the Prophet (PBUH) Abraham (PBUH) or Adam (PBUH) built it. They face toward the Kabah during the daily prayers. The Muslim worship places, mosques, are built in a direction so that people can face toward the Kabah.

Muslims visit the Kabah during their pilgrimage. As part of their worship, they go around the Kabah by reciting prayers, and sit around it. Muslims view the Kabah as a symbol of respect.[30] In the beginning of Islam, early Muslims used to pray toward Jerusalem as part of the Abrahamic religion. Later, the permanent location of direction for prayers changed with an order from Allah سبحانه وتعالى in the Quran, and this has become the Kabah.

Praying toward the Kabah five times a day gives Muslims the understanding of being directionally oriented in their lives. In other words, in their hometown or while they are travelling, they should be aware of where the east or north is if they are living in America, since these directions form the great circle to the Kabah.

The symbol of the Kabah, as a solid structure or building, establishes the concept of a sacred and sensible structure that the Prophet (PBUH) Abraham (PBUH) had built. The Prophet (PBUH) Abraham (PBUH) is the symbol of worshipping one Allah سبحانه وتعالى in Islam. The Prophet (PBUH) Abraham (PBUH) built this structure or repaired it in order

---

30. Shai'r in Ar.

for people to worship Allah سبحانه وتعالى and perform their pilgrimage at a sacred place. Some non-Muslims may think that Muslims are worshipping the building, but on the contrary, it is built by Prophet Abraham (PBUH) as the representer of monotheism. Muslims don't worship the Kabah but they use it for directional purposes and they turn toward it to establish unity and structure for their prayers. This direction is ordered by Allah سبحانه وتعالى. There is a fine line between idol worship and regarding something as a symbol of the sacred. According to one of the narrations from the Rasulullah ﷺ, Kabah is the first temple of worship on earth to worship One and only Allah سبحانه وتعالى.[10] In Islamic legal and theological system, a life of a human is greater than the Kabah. This indicates that for Muslims Kabah is just a sacred object.

MECCA, SAUDI ARABIA—Muslim pilgrims from all around the world circling around the Kabah on January 29, 2017.

What are the similarities and differences between Islam, Judaism, and Christianity?

Comparing Islam with Christianity, Judaism, and other Religions

According to the Abrahamic religions, Allah سبحانه وتعالى is one. Allah سبحانه وتعالى has different names and attributes. Allah سبحانه وتعالى is the Merciful. Allah سبحانه وتعالى is the Loving and Loved one. Allah سبحانه

وتعالى is the Preserver, the Real King, and the Knower. There are many attributes of Allah سبحانه وتعالى. Although "He" is used to refer to Allah سبحانه وتعالى, Allah سبحانه وتعالى is neither He nor She.

Christianity, Judaism, and Islam are classified as Abrahamic religions. These three religions all believe Abraham (PBUH) as their common ancestor or prophet and accept his teachings. Abraham (PBUH) is the symbol of believing in One Allah سبحانه وتعالى. Therefore, Christianity, Judaism, and Islam are all monotheistic religions. Along with their substantial commonalities, they have also some differences. Some of them are summarized in the table following.

	Judaism	Christianity	Islam
Belief in Oneness and Uniqueness of سبحانه وتعالى	✓	✓	✓
Trinity		✓	
Belief in Prophets/Messengers	✓	✓	✓
Belief in Afterlife	✓	✓	✓
Belief in Accountability	✓	✓	✓
Belief in Angels	✓	✓	✓
Divinity of Jesus		✓	
Prophethood or Messengership of Jesus		✓	✓
Jesus as the Messiah		✓	✓
Miracle Birth of Jesus		✓	✓
Second Coming of Jesus		✓	✓
Original Sin		✓	
Moses as the Messenger of Allah	✓	✓	✓
Abraham as the Messenger of Allah	✓	✓	✓

Source: Dr. Y. J. Kumek

Although the check mark denotes the commonalities among the three religions mentioned in the above table, how they understand and interpret each shared and common belief can be different from each other.

Some of the common shared incidents are very similarly mentioned in the Quran, the Old and New Testaments. For example, the narratives about Moses (PBUH), David (PBUH), Abraham (PBUH), Jonah, Soloman (PBUH), Noah (PBUH), the creation of Adam (PBUH) and his relation with Satan, the creation of the universe in six days, and many others. Jesus (PBUH) is accepted as a prophet by the Muslims, because Jesus (PBUH) came with a message and book from Allah سبحانه وتعالى to revive and reinstate the original message from Allah سبحانه وتعالى. In Islam, Adam (PBUH) is a noble prophet of Allah سبحانه وتعالى in Islam. Adam (PBUH) and Eve were sent to earth not as a punishment but for a mission of being close to Allah سبحانه وتعالى with their offspring. Therefore, their coming down to earth was a spiritual ascension not a spiritual descent. Therefore, there is no original sin in Islam.

Are the Muslims in America and Europe different?

Islam in the West

Islam has become a critical religion in America and Europe due to various reasons. Islam in America and Europe has different populations that form the identity of Muslims such as immigrant Muslims, second-generation Muslims, and converted Muslims. The immigrant Muslims constitute those who migrated from Muslim majority countries. Second-generation Muslims are the children of the immigrant Muslims who were born in America or Europe. They try to combine their Western culture with the native cultures of their parents. The convert Muslims are those who adopt Islam as a new way of life. Some famous Muslims are Muhammad Ali and Mike Tyson (boxers), Cat Stevens (singer, with his new name Yusuf Islam), Dr. Oz (Medical Doctor), and Kareem Abdul-Jabbar (NBA basketball player).

The immigrant Muslims who migrated to the West have been establishing their institutions, and being part of the social life. Their children are becoming part of the educational system forming the identities of "American Muslims" and "European Muslims." Especially, this identity is more dominant in America where there is no single prevailing nationality in the country.

Muslim institutions are either predominantly ethnic-based or a mixture of ethnicities. In the places where a Muslim ethnicity is dominant, it is expected to see a mosque to reflect the culture of that ethnicity in the understanding of the religion. For example, in an Arab or Indian culturally majority mosque, it is common to see women wearing black, colorful, or traditional clothes. On the other hand, the mosques with attendees of Bosnian or Turkish culture would mostly have casual dress while attending to the mosque. In some of the metropolitan cities, it is easy to see the very mixture of different cultures and ethnicities in the worship places and services.

An annual celebration prayer ('eid) can be in any spacious indoor or outdoor place. An example of this prayer is in a basketball stadium in Windsor, Canada, as presented below. The mixture of different ethnicities is very vivid in the picture below. Muslims generally rent huge spaces, such as stadiums to hold thousands of people in their locality during their annual prayer.

What is the culture of Islam?

Customs and Culture

Women and men tend to reflect their cultural preference in implantation of the understanding of Islamic teachings. This reflection can be in worship places, social life, and professional environments. Islamic teachings are not there to change the culture or tradition[31] as long as it does not conflict basic premises such as belief in One Creator, justice, free choice, and individual rights.

---

31. Urf.

Are Muslims violent?

Violence

Islam, an Abrahamic religion whose name literally means "peace and submission," and Muslims, who adopt these teachings, continuously and popularly face a challenge from violent elements using their name. According to Muslim sources,[27] a small but loud group is committing inhuman actions of violence in the name of their faith. According to them, modern media have been overlooking the voices of the millions of Muslims who are horrified by these events.

The Quran and the practices of the Prophet of Islam, Prohet Muhammad (PBUH), harshly warn against any type of behavior that provokes fear and loathing. The Quran and hadith, scholarly records of the Prophet's (PBUH) actions and reactions, as well as the works of Islamic scholars, very clearly condemn all sorts of violent persecution. These are the textual sources of Islam's teachings. According to Muslims, Muhammad (PBUH) is a role model for all Muslims, and sincere efforts to emulate his character are an important aspect of Islam. He strongly opposed malicious violence and his views were based upon the Quranic verse that equates the killing of an innocent person with killing all humanity [Quran 5:32].

As mentioned by Karen Armstrong,[8] the Rasulullah ﷺ clearly demonstrated respect for ethnic and religious diversity. To give an example, he stood to honor the funeral parade of a Jewish man, and by doing so, taught people to respect humans for their moral attributes, regardless of their faith. He also allowed Christians of Najran to perform their prayers right in his mosque in Madina which exemplifies religious tolerance. Prophet Muhammad's (PBUH) guests were from all ethnic and religious (Christians, Jews, Zoroastrians, and polytheists) backgrounds. All were respected and treated honorably in his presence. He offered non-binding advice to all communities. Despite the current wave of destruction in the name of religion, the relics of ancient religions and communities of non-Muslims were safe in Muslim lands for hundreds of years under Islamic rule. This testifies to the respect Islamic peoples have had for the pre-Muslim past and to the sublime and accommodating nature of the religion.[28]

So how is it possible that a religion that so strongly promotes peace and dialogue can be manipulated to such a degree that vulnerable young Muslims are drawn into violence? There have been many historical incidents where self-proclaimed religious leaders manipulated the emotions of the ignorant masses for a political objective. These orators speak charismatically in the name of Allah سبحانه وتعالى, to provoke feelings of fear and guilt. Catastrophic events followed. This was true for Islam, Christianity, and Judaism. Using passages out of context from holy books and exploiting them to incite violent behavior is not a new occurrence, and the Quran is not the first of the sacred texts to be abused in this way.

"Read" is the first verse revealed to Rasulullah ﷺ [96:1]. Education offers us the possibility of resolving many human problems including the mistaken views of violence in Islam. Muslims believe that there are currently far too few opportunities to expand one's knowledge about Islam beyond the news industry, which often sensationalizes violent actions of some Muslims, committed in the name of Islam. According to some emerging scholars in the West,[17] this education should focus upon the original teachings of the Quran and genuine practices of Prophet Muhammad (PBUH) with their accurate interpretations. There is already overwhelming consensus in Islamic scholarly traditions against violence. Therefore, Muslim youth should be equipped with these foundations to help distinguish between the original teachings of Islam and feigned ideas, and prevent any type of deceptive manipulation.

Islam consists of a diversity of sects and perspectives and all, save a few, condemn violence. Muslims are increasing their efforts in the West to take leadership in educating their communities with the peaceful teachings of Islam. There is an increasing and positive awareness toward religious education of the possible vulnerable groups in the West by the civil groups. The government agencies regularly support these initiatives of education. These agencies have positively increased their efforts to connect with Muslim grassroots organizations to increase the awareness of the horrible effects of violence.

What is Islamic Law?

Law, Society, and Politics

There are detailed guidelines of worship and social and family relationships for an ethical and peaceful life in Islam. The fundamental methodology to establish these guidelines is by studying the Quran, by the sayings and practices of the Rasulullah [32] by the consensus of the scholars on a matter, and by using logic and critical thinking. It is important to understand the systemization and canonization of these methods and later formation of different legal schools or madhabs[33] in Islamic history. These guidelines are markedly based on basic universal values such as not to transgress the rights of other humans, animals, trees, or the environment. The goal of these guidelines and rulings is to establish balance as practiced by the Prophet (PBUH). Historically, depending on the time and location, volumes of books have been written to systematize the teachings of the Quran and the sayings and practices of the Rasulullah. This continually updated systemization, such as the constitution of a country, helped the following generations understand the occurrences with their relation to the context, time, person, and their specificity and generalizability of the occurrences. This systemization is called Islamic law.[34] One of the motivating reasons to establish guidelines after the demise of the Prophet (PBUH) and earlier generations was to prevent literal and wrong interpretations of the Quran and sayings and practices of the Rasulullah. As mentioned for religious texts and scriptures, following the letter (scripture) but not spirit of the letter could be deadly.[17] This saying indicates the importance of not following religious scriptures literally but with scholarly, contextual, and sound interpretations.

---

32. Referred to as hadith and Sunnah.
33. Such as Hanafi, Shafii, Maliki, Hanbali schools.
34. Referred to as Fiqh by the Muslims or mostly Shariah by the Westerners.

What is Sufism?

Sufism

Sufism is the deeper understanding and practice of one's relationship with Allah سبحانه وتعالى. According to some Sufis, people are spirits in physical bodies.[22] A person who establishes an intimate relationship with Allah سبحانه وتعالى sets a goal on a spiritual journey to please Allah سبحانه وتعالى. This lifelong struggle, or journey until death is named, or characterized as, Sufism by the Westerners and called "Tasawwuf" by some Muslims. Sufism describes the structural outline of this spiritual journey; although some of the Muslim sholars may not be in favor of this type of characterization. People have a need to fulfill the spiritual hunger. If the person doesn't care about spiritual sustenance from a pure source then the soul will take it from a poisonous source.

A Sufi teacher can be viewed as a personal spiritual trainer. The Sufi teacher's[35] goal is to teach and diagnose a person's sickness of the heart, soul, and other spiritual faculties. With practice and knowledge, the person becomes a better human being in the sight of Allah سبحانه وتعالى and for other humans, and for living and non-living things. For example, one of the Sufi Masters say that

> "I don't throw a scratch paper in the garbage with other garbage materials. I fold it nicely put it in a separate place due to my respect to knowledge, to the tree that the paper was made of and to the Creator who gave all those for my service."

The actions and thought processes of Sufis some or most of the time may be seen as not the norm or may be viewed as extraordinary by others. The concept of ethical and spiritual perfection is summarized with one of the famous Sufi sayings, "Good deeds of pious are the disobedience of the elect ones."[29] This means that every person's spiritual journey is individualized and there is no end to climb up in the spiritual journey. An example of this can be of two students. One student comes late to the class and it is good that he still came to the class even though it was

---

35. Murshid in terminology.

late for the teacher. On the other hand, for a punctual and good student, coming late to the class can be an act of disobedience to the teacher.

Some Sufis interpret the death as the wedding day of the loved and the beloved,[24] meaning the mystical Union of the person and Allah سبحانه وتعالى. Some of the essentials in Sufism are a good teacher and good company. These are the two main vehicles to remind the main teaching of Sufism in the journey to the Loved, Allah سبحانه وتعالى. The discourses of the Loved, Allah سبحانه وتعالى, is all the type of genuine conversations, experiences, reflections, and feelings that would help the spiritual traveler to get closer and closer to Allah سبحانه وتعالى until the person dies. Any type of unrelated indulgence, conversations, experience, thoughts, reflections, and feelings are considered null and insignificant if it is not serving this purpose of intimate relationship with the Loved, Allah سبحانه وتعالى.

What is the role of women in Islam?

Women

It is important to analyze the change of the status of women in the society before and after Islam. Before Islam, in the desert Arabian region women were much oppressed and were exploited mostly as a commodity. Female infanticide was very common, which is also mentioned in the Quran [81:9]. Women were not able to inherit and did not have any public respect or position, with very few exceptions.[8] With the advent of Islam, one of the main criticisms raised against Prophet Muhammad (PBUH) by his contemporaries was his liberal expressions about women. One of the Rasulullah ﷺ's early critics said, "Look at Muhammad, he is changing all our values. He is even giving rights to the women."[8]

After Islam, women gained important roles in the society and family. The practice of the Rasulullah ﷺ was very encouraging and supporting to the self-stance of women in the society. His wife, Aisha, was a very prominent intellectual. She later became the commander in chief (top general) of the army after the demise of the Prophet (PBUH) in a critical war in Muslim history.[30] This was totally novel in that society a woman leading an army. Among many, another example is today's most prominent chain of institutions in Islamic sciences in Egypt, Al-Azhar. It established by a woman. Currently, every year, thousands of students graduate from this institution. This institution has a very high reputation among Muslims and non-Muslims.

Although there are very strong teachings to prevent the abuse of women and the encouragement for minority representations, the cultural expectations sometimes intervene with religious teachings and unfortunately one can still see a lot of issues revolving around women's rights in society and family life today. One of the famous sayings of the Rasulullah ﷺ which frequently circulates in Muslim sermons is that, "The best of you is the one who is in best treatment of his family (wife)."[10] There is an increasing movement of especially educated women both in the West and other parts of the world challenging androcentric and patriarchal interpretation of religious teachings. The emergence of female religious scholars is promising to be a positive effort toward removing cultural and masculine subjective interpretations from the primary teachings of the Quran and the hadith.[31]

In family life, it is understood that the financial responsibilities are required to be fulfilled by the man, as suggested by the Islamic legal law. The wife has the right to work but it is not required for her to contribute to the family expenses including her own expenses according to the Islamic law. If she contributes to the family expenses, then it is considered charity on her part although she is not obliged to. In other words, the Islamic teachings put the responsibility of financial maintenance of the house on the man. She is not required to contribute to the household expenses.

In gender interpretation of women, it is assumed and recognized that women are natural givers with a lot of sacrifice in child upbringing and their gender-related needs can be different than men. Therefore, sacred legal responsibilities of a woman are less compared to men. For example, a woman on her menstruation cycle does not need to pray and fast. She is not required to go to mosque on Fridays compared to men. It is required for men but optional or discretionary for women to attend the Friday sermons.

In Muslim discourses of the gender, a woman in Islam is generally depicted with her spiritual and physical beauty. Therefore, the textual and oral discourses emerge to prevent the abuse of the woman physically and spiritually. One can find these explicit teachings in the verses of the Quran and in the sayings of the Rasulullah ﷺ. Therefore, Muslim women practice the Islamic teachings of the dress code in order to implement modesty in their personal life and not to be exploited physically due to their gender. One of the examples that Muslim women take as their role model is the mother of Jesus (PBUH), Virgin Mary (PBUH). They believe that she had a similar way of dress code to implement modesty. Therefore, they emulate Virgin Mary (PBUH) in every aspect.[32]

In a court system, the woman can bring her friend to witness together on a matter whereas a man can assume that responsibility by himself alone. Muslims argue that witnessing is a responsibility not a privilege. In the Quran, Allah سبحانه وتعالى puts the limits, for example, for the man not to divorce his wife during her menstrual cycle due to her sickness.

According to emerging need with the new Muslim scholarship, especially due to diaspora, Muslims should follow the law of the land. If the law requires them to perform something unlawful according to the Quran, they should migrate to another land and seek another residence. With this perspective, Muslim women in the West rationalize the multiple wife discretionary of a husband as given in the special cases. Therefore, Muslim men should not break the law by having more than one wife if the law does not allow polygamy. According to normative exegesis of the Quran, the sacred text advises monogamy. Exceptional cases for polygamy were given when women especially need protection in the tribal societies through marriage. Another example that is given by the Islamic legalists is that if the wife is sick and the man wants to get married with another person he may have a valid reason. He can still take care of his sick wife without getting divorced.

How are contemporary social ethics issues viewed?

Social Ethics

One can look at today's social ethics issues in Islam as well as such things as drugs, alcohol, abortion, LGBT, dating, marriage, extramarital affairs, and many others.

As a general rule of methodology,[36] Islamic ethical and legal guidelines implicitly and explicitly are intended to benefit the individual, the society, and the living and non-living things at-large on the earth and in the universe. These very basic principles are historically established methodologies with the teachings of the Quran, sayings and practices of the Rasulullah ﷺ and later, with the institutionalized schools of law and practice.[37] Some of the underlining basic principles are protecting individual rights, freedom, honor, and property. Then, the benefit of the society[38] at-large can occur, but without transgressing these basic individual rights. There have always been the positive and constructive friction of this hardly balanced pendulum, swinging between the individual and social benefits when decisions and enforcements prevail. In other words, in Islamic social ethics, one cannot harm or kill one person to benefit one hundred people. One cannot pursue a virtuous goal with evil means. In other words, all the steps to achieve a virtuous end should also be virtuous.

In the personal affairs, the type of benefit or transgression is classified into two categories: the issues related to the individual and Allah سبحانه وتعالى, and the issues related to the individual and other humans and beings. One can call this vertical, transcendent relation with Allah سبحانه وتعالى and horizontal relationship with humans. Everyone has the free will to choose what they want to believe and what they want to do. The Quran repeats and highlights the concept of transgression or wrong.[39] Transgression or relationship emerges in two types: vertical (related to the Creator) and horizontal (related to the people). Transgression against the Creator does not bear any accountability in this world. This transgression is mainly not recognizing Allah سبحانه وتعالى as the Creator and consequently not appreciating Allah's سبحانه وتعالى favors. The second type of transgression is against human dignity on social justice. It could involve invidious discrimination by race, ethnicity, or religion. The Quran suggests law enforcement measures to remove this type of transgression. Some social Islamic scholars, such as Fazlur Rahman,[33] suggest that legal rulings for law enforcement could

---

36. Usul.
37. Called Mazhabs.
38. Urf or Maslaha.
39. Zulm.

be secular as long as the laws are fair, just, and transparent which is the essential objective of the Quranic legal system.[40] As the result of both types of offenses, according to Quranic teachings, the person in reality wrongs, oppresses, or transgresses, himself or herself.[41] There is no compulsion in the choice of belief or religion as mentioned in the verses of the Quran [2:256]. Islam has in some ways similar and in some ways different understanding of the social ethic issues with other Abrahamic religions: normative Christianity and normative Judaism.

In these rulings, for example, drugs can be used for medical purposes. Although limited consumption of alcohol can have benefits, due to the weakness of the individual's self-control and its possible adversary effects to the society, the rulings discourage and try to stop usage of alcohol. The formation of a baby in the mother's womb and its timelines are implicitly and explicitly expressed in the Quran. Therefore, the cases of abortion are considered individually case by case depending on the medical need, the stage of the trimester of the baby, and the reasons of abortion if it is a choice without any reason. In Islamic legal normative books written centuries ago,[42] there are extensive sections about similar cases of LGBT. The arguments can take each case separately especially with the medical cases of "khunnas" similar somehow to what is defined as LGBT today. In the cases of extramarital affairs, the guidelines are present to establish fair, reputable, and healthy societies based on healthy families. Marital and kinship relationships are to protect the rights of children and women but at the same time encouraging men to establish long-term happy and mutual beneficial relationships for all the stakeholders.

In all of the above cases and in other social ethics issues, the normative Islamic understanding is that there is no hate to the sinner but there is a disapproval and dislike to the action.

---

40. Shari'ah
41. Nafs- wa lakinna anfusahum yazlimun in Arabic repeated in different parts of the Quran.
42. By Imam Abu Hanifah, Shafili Malik, and in their commentaries such as in Hidayah.[711]

What is the status of art, education, and science in Islam?

Art, Education, and Science

One can observe the reflections of Islamic art in different parts of the social, educational, and professional life. Calligraphy and linguistic art are examples of two popular types. One can observe the stylistic writings of the verses and name of Allah سبحانه وتعالى in the walls of mosques and in picture frames in the houses, cars, stores, and offices of the Muslims. One can observe different Islamic monuments, temples, and prayer carpets reflecting the culture with Islamic motifs.

Linguistic art can be observed in the traditional composition of poems and writings especially inspired from the words, styles, and teachings of the Quran and sayings of the Prophets (PBUH). One should have knowledge of semantics, knowledge of figures of speech like similes and metaphors, and knowledge of the rhetoric to understand the phase constructions, implicit and explicit meanings which reveal the beauty of the language and its implications. In Muslim countries, there is a substantial habit of listening to the Quranic recitation similar to listening to music.

In Islam, education is very crucial. There are a lot of prophetic sayings which emphasize being educated. In one of the famous sayings of the Rasulullah ﷺ: "For Satan, it is 1,000 times more difficult to give temptations and false guidance to an educated scholar than to an uneducated naive worshipper.[26]" This teaching especially encourages Muslims to be educated in their religion and science,s not to be blind followers. According to this saying of the Prophet (PBUH), a Allah سبحانه وتعالى-conscious scholar has a higher level than a pious worshipper who is less educated. In one other saying of the Rasulullah ﷺ, it is mentioned that for every Muslim it is required to learn.[34]

The Quran especially emphasizesreflection, and critical thinking about scientific events and nature in order to find Allah سبحانه وتعالى. The Quran states that the scholars who have knowledge and education are the real believers that have fear, respect, awe, and love of Allah سبحانه وتعالى. Historically, Muslims did not have a problem with science, rather they were encouraged to look for different cosmological, microscopic, and macroscopic events with scientific knowledge due to the encouragement of many verses in the Quran. One can find many verses of the Quran about different disciplines of natural, humanities, and social sciences such as embryology, biology, astronomy, zoology, chemistry, sociology, logic, philosophy, and literature.[35]

A window in Morocco in a historical mosque.

What is Halal?

A Muslim's Diet, Permissible and Impermissible

Halal is permissible and haram is impermissible in food and other religious legal categorizations. Therefore, one can find "halal" labels in Muslims' food items. The Muslims do not eat any animal sacrificed for other than Allah سبحانه وتعالى. Similar to Jewish tradition, Muslims don't eat pork and wild animals. There is an understanding that the effect of the food can have an effect, not only on the physical body, but also on the metaphysical faculties of a person.[24] A person engaged in permissible, halal, will find easiness in one's prayers and following the commands of Allah سبحانه وتعالى. On the contrary, the person who is eating and dealing with the impermissible may not feel the same desire to establish relationship with Allah سبحانه وتعالى and perform prayers. This person can become unethical in one's relationships with people and Allah سبحانه وتعالى. The number of impermissible items are a few compared to the permissible items in Islam. Although one can find a lot of books on the wisdom and the possible reasons of impermissible items, Muslims are required to distinguish between halal (permissible) with haram (impermissible) with submissive attitude to Allah سبحانه وتعالى.

In social life, there are impermissible and permissible items as well according to Islamic value system. It is permissible and commendable to loan money to someone but it is impermissible to get interest from it. It is impermissible to gamble and drink alcohol. It is impermissible and a huge sin to kill an innocent person, lie, cheat, backbite, and slander. It is not permissible being full while the neighbor is hungry.

If a Muslim performs any of the impermissible actions, then this person is classified as a sinner. The accountability of the person is between this person and Allah سبحانه وتعالى. This person can ask repentance from Allah سبحانه وتعالى any time before death. If the transgression or evil is related to others' rights, then this person should seek the means of forgiveness in this world from these individuals in addition to asking forgiveness from Allah سبحانه وتعالى.

PART 2
SELECTED PASSAGES
FROM THE QURAN
WITH INTERPRETED MEANINGS

The Names of Chapters in the Quran

1	Al-Fatiha	The Opening
2	Al-Baqarah	The Cow Story
3	Al-'Imran	The Family of Imran
4	An-Nisa'	The Women
5	Al-Ma'idah	The Feast
6	Al-An'am	The Cattle
7	Al-A'raf	The Elevated Places
8	Al-Anfal	Voluntary Gifts
9	At-Taubah	The Repentance
10	Yunus	Jonah
11	Hud	Hud
12	Yusuf	Joseph
13	Ar-Ra'd	The Thunder
14	Ibrahim	Abraham
15	Al-Hijr	The Place of Rocks
16	An-Nahl	The Bee
17	Al- Isra	The Night Journey
18	Al-Kahf	The Cave
19	Maryam	Jesus's Mother Virgin Mary
20	Ta Ha	The Letters T, H
21	Al-Anbiya'	The Prophets
22	Al-Hajj	The Pilgrimage
23	Al-Mu'minun	The Believers
24	An-Nur	The Light
25	Al-Furqan	The Separator
26	Ash-Shu'ara'	The Poets
27	An-Naml	The Ant
28	Al-Qasas	The Narrative
29	Al-'Ankabut	The Spider
30	Ar-Rum	The Romans

31	Luqman	Luqman, The Wise
32	As-Sajdah	The Prostration
33	Al-Ahzab	The Allies
34	Al-Saba'	The Sheba
35	Al-Fatir	The Originator
36	Ya Sin	The Letters Y, S
37	As-Saffat	Those Ranging in Ranks
38	Sad	The Letter S
39	Az-Zumar	The Companies
40	Al-Mu'min	The Believer
41	HaMim	The Letters H, M
42	Ash-Shura	The Counsel
43	Az-Zukhruf	The Gold
44	Ad-Dukhan	The Smoke
45	Al-Jathiyah	The Kneeling
46	Al-Ahqaf	The Sandhills
47	Muhammad	Muhammad
48	Al-Fath	The Victory
49	Al-Hujurat	The Apartments
50	Qaf	The letter Q
51	Ad-Dhariyat	The Scatterers
52	At-Tur	The Mountain
53	An-Najm	The Star
54	Al-Qamar	The Moon
55	Ar-Rahman	The All Merciful
56	Al-Waqi'ah	The Event
57	Al-Hadid	The Iron
58	Al-Mujadilah	The Woman in Appeal
59	Al-Hashr	The Gathering
60	Al-Mumtahanah	The Examined
61	As-Saff	The Ranks
62	Al-Jumu'ah	The Friday Congregation

63	Al-Munafiqun	The Hypocrites
64	At-Taghabun	Mutual Loss
65	At-Talaq	Divorce
66	At-Tahrim	The Prohibition
67	Al-Mulk	The Authority
68	Al-Qalam	The Pen
69	Al-Haqqah	The Reality
70	Al-Ma'arij	The Ways of Ascent
71	Nuh	Noah
72	Al-Jinn	The Unseen Beings
73	Al-Muzzammil	The Covered One
74	Al-Muddaththir	The Cloaked One
75	Al-Qiyamah	The Resurrection
76	Al-Insan	The Man
77	Al-Mursalat	Those Sent Forth
78	An-Naba'	The News
79	An-Nazi'at	The Pullers
80	'Abasa	The One Who Frowned
81	At-Takwir	The Folding Up
82	Al-Infitar	The Cleaving
83	mutafifeen	The Fraud
84	Al-Inshiqaq	The Massive Explosion
85	Al-Buruj	The Sea of Stars
86	At-Tariq	The Morning Star
87	Al-A'laa	The Most High
88	Al-Ghashiyah	The Overwhelming Event
89	Al-Fajr	The Daybreak
90	Al-Balad	The City
91	Ash-Shams	The Sun
92	Al-Lail	The Night
93	Ad-Duha	The Morning Hour

94	Al-Inshirah	The Chest Expansion
95	At-Tin	The Fig
96	Al-'Alaq	The Embryo
97	Al-Qadr	The Power
98	Al-Bayyinah	The Clear Proof
99	Al-Zilzal	The Earthquake
100	Al-'Adiyat	The Raiders
101	Al-Qari'ah	The Calamity
102	At-Takathur	The Greed
103	Al-'Asr	The Time
104	Al-Humazah	The Slanderer
105	Al-Fil	The Elephant
106	Al-Quraish	The Tribe of Quraish
107	Al-Ma'un	The Small Kindness
108	Al-Kauthar	The Abundance
109	Al-Kafirun	The Ungrateful Ones
110	An-Nasr	The Help
111	Al-Lahab	The Flame
112	Al-Ikhlas	The Unity
113	Al-Falaq	The Dawn
114	An- Nas	The Mankind

The above table presents the chapter numbers and names of the Quran with their original Arabic and their translated possible meanings chosen among different possibilities. In this book, at least one verse from each chapter of the Quran is selected to introduce the unfamiliar English reader to the main sacred text of Islam. Instead of using original above chapter names, the selected themes of the verses were carried in the titles for each chapter accompanied with the original chapter numbers. The first number in the brackets denotes the above chapter numbers and the second number denotes the verse numbers within the chapter.

Table of Different Names of the Quran

Below is a table of different names and attributes of the Quran which are mentioned in the Quran itself in different chapters and verses [39] [40]. In other words, the Quran calls itself with different names in its own text. Each name of the Quran occurs in the Quran with different repetitive numbers. The most repeated name is "the Quran" which can be translated as "the one that is read a lot." The next recurring name is "the Book." In Islamic theology, the revelation is a book, the universe is a book, and the human being is a book. All the books triangulate together and they are complementary[25]. The next frequent name is "the Descended Revelation from Allah سبحانه وتعالى" which is repeated constantly to tell the reader that this sacred Book is not made up by a human such as Muhammad (PBUH), but revealed and descended to humans from Allah سبحانه وتعالى. The next repetitive name is "the Reminder" that the Quran is a reminder for the one who is wise and can take advice. The next repeated name is "the Right Guidance" which the Quran is a guidance for the seeker. The next recurrent name is "the truth" that is reiterated in the Quran to remind the reader that all content of the Quran is the truth and there is no doubt. The next frequent name is "the Confirming Scripture of the Bible: the Gospel, the Psalms, and the Torah, and Previous Scriptures Sent by Allah سبحانه وتعالى" which tells the reader that the message in the Quran is not something new but confirms the original messages of the previous scriptures sent by Allah سبحانه وتعالى such as the Bible, Torah, and others. The below table presents different names of the Quran presented in the Quran itself with the number of occurrences in the text.

	Different Names of the Quran in the Quran and their Translation		Number of occurrences in the Quran
1	Al-Kitab	The Book	27
2	Mubin	The Clarifier	5
3	Al-Quran	The Quran	30
4	Karim	Honorable, Noble	1
5	Kalam Allah	The Word of Allah	1
6	Nur	Sacred Light	3
7	Al-Huda	The Guidance	11
8	Rahmah	Mercy	5
9	Al-Furqan	The Criterion	3
10	As-Shifa	The Healer	3
11	Maw'iza	Admonition	3
12	Dhikr	The Reminder	12
13	Mubarak	Blessed	4
14	Al'i	The Exalted	1
15	Al-Hikmah	The Wisdom	1
16	Al-Hakim	The Full of Wisdom	4
17	Al-Muhaymin	The Guardian of the Bible: the Gospel, the Psalms, and the Torah	1
18	Musaddiq	Conforming Scripture of the Bible: the Gospel, the Psalms, and the Torah	7
19	Hablillah	The Rope of Allah	1
20	Sirat al mustaqim	The Straight Path	1
21	Qayyim	Straight Guidance	1
22	Qawl	The Word	2
23	Al-Fasl	The Separator	1
24	Nabaun Azam	Supreme Message	2
25	Ahsan ul Hadith	The Best Message	1
26	Mathani	The Repeated	1
27	Mutashabih	Consistent in Itself	1

28	Tanzil	The Descended Revelation	14
29	Ruh	The Book which Gives Life to Faith	1
30	Wahy	The Revelation	4
31	Arabi	In Arabic	6
32	Basair	The Discernment	2
33	Bayan	The Final Statement	1
34	Ilm	Unlimited Knowledge	2
35	Haqq	The Truth, True	10
36	Hadi	The Guide	3
37	Ajab	Wonderful	1
38	Tadhkira	Admonition, Reminder	3
39	Urwatul Wuthqa	The Firm Handhold	1
40	Sidq	The Truth	2
41	Al-Adl	The Justice	1
42	AmrAllah	The Commandment of Allah	1
43	Munadi	Inviter to the Faith	1
44	Bushra	Glad Tidings	4
45	Majid	The Glorious	2
46	Zabur	The Scripture	1
47	Bashir	Herald of Glad Tidings	2
48	Nadhir	The Warner	1
49	Aziz	The Mighty	1
50	Balagh	The Sufficient Message	2
51	Qasas	Narratives	1
52	Suhuf	The Scripture	2
53	Mukarrama	The Honored	1
54	Marfua	Exalted	1
55	Mutahhara	Kept Pure	2

Note on Transliteration and Translated Interpretive Meanings

This book uses a contextual translation approach as explained in detail in the appendix about the translation technique. In this method, the translator tries to give an intended meaning of the verse by analyzing the traditional and contemporary exegetical meanings[43] in order to carry it into today's everyday English language. Although it is not easy to give interpretive meanings to Quranic verses, my effort and intention was to decrease the barriers of understandability and clarity for some of the verses of the Quran. It is well known that the difficulty of translation with interpretive meanings is due to many genres of the Quranic Arabic, the content, the style, the context, the audience, the inclusivity and the exclusivity, the legality, the clear and implicit meanings, and others.

The available and popular English translations were analyzed. Here is the methodology that I followed: In most of the verses, in the beginning I tried to translate without looking at other translations. After the translation was completed, I reviewed other renderings in other translations for the selected verses. Most of the time due to the archaic, non-contextual, unclear, and improper choice of words of the available translations, I preferred to use the interpreted exegetical contemporary as this methodology is detailed in the appendix section of this book.

In these interpreted meanings, the selected translations in this book may show an effort to minimize the incorrect renderings about Allah سبحانه وتعالى due to the figurative language in the original language of Arabic when translated into the target language of English. Some scholars can refer this as the method of "tanzih," knowing first who Allah سبحانه وتعالى is not, then, knowing who Allah سبحانه وتعالى is. For example, below is an excerpt from this book for the translation of the word "Rabb" which comes frequently in the Quran:

> Rabb is translated as "Allah, the Originator, Upholder and Maintainer" for the chapter of Opening (Fatiha). The classical translations [5][6][4][3][2][7] for Rabb in other texts generally prefer

---

43. Tafsir in Arabic

the word "Lord" in English except M. Asad's translation. [1] Lord
in classical English can refer to the authority and ownership with
slavery with negative embedded meanings [8]. Also, in Christian
theology, Lord can usually be used for Jesus, which may cause
confusion for the unfamiliar reader. One of the common words
in daily usage of this word is related to the owner of a property
referred to as the landlord which can have reductive meanings
for the general English reader. Oppositely, in Arabic, Rabb
has many meanings such as upbringing, nourishing, teaching,
making order, upkeeping, caregiving, controlling, safeguarding,
and maintaining with love, mercy, and care. Therefore, the best
example of this can be the usage when parents have a relationship
with their child with all these qualities of the word rabb with
love, mercy, and care. In this text, depending on the context,
different attributes of Allah embedded in the attribute of Rabb
are chosen and used. M. Asad's translation [1] uses Sustainer as
the translation of Rabb, which is a very good attempt to change
the traditional vocabulary for this word, but I think it is not
sufficient to include all the meanings of Rabb depending on the
context.

I had the intention and effort of translating all the words into English to
eliminate alienation for the unfamiliar and general readers. For example,
the name of "Allah" is translated as Allah سبحانه وتعالى to minimize the
confusion although it may not give the exact meaning. The Rasulullah
ﷺ is sometimes referred to as the Prophet. I tried to avoid parenthesis in
the translations to make the text user-friendly for the unfamiliar readers
of the scriptures. To increase the flow, the proper adverbs are placed
within the intended and contextual meaning of the original language.
I tried to give immediate contextual apparent explicit meanings (zahir)
compared to their implicit (batin) ones although it is always arguable by
the exegetical scholars what can be explicit and implicit.

I want to make very clear as it is outlined in all the translations of the
Quran that the translations are the interpreted meanings of the Quran.
The original Quran is in Arabic. It is very careful and collectively agreed
within the Islamic theology that the translations are not called the
Quran, the sacred revelation. Therefore, one should realize this very fine

point that this book is not the Quran, therefore it is titled as "Selected verses of the Quran with interpreted meanings." It is always encouraged and stipulated in practice and scholarly endeavors to learn the language of Arabic as well as the scriptural sciences to appropriate the meanings of the Quran.

It is interesting to note for the English reader that one of the names or attributes of the Quran mentioned in the Quran itself, is al-Muhaymin or al-Musaddiq. Al-Muhaymin can mean the guardian of the Bible: the New and Old Testaments. This means that the role of the Quran is to ensure and acknowledge that Allah سبحانه وتعالى sent the Gospel to Jesus, Torah to Moses (PBUH), and Psalms to David (PBUH). Therefore, the Quran reassures in many of its verses that the the Bible: Psalms, Gospels, and Torah were the revelations from Allah سبحانه وتعالى. Also, al-Mussadiq is the name of the Quran which can be translated as the Confirming Scripture of the Bible: the New and Old Testaments. The Quran confirms the similar teachings in the Bible: the Gospel, the Psalms, and the Torah especially in the scopes of the belief such as believing in One Allah سبحانه وتعالى, and accountability in the afterlife, and in the scopes of ethical behavior such as the actualization of justice in personal and social levels.

Although there are minimal transliterated words, this book uses a simplified version of the standard academic transliteration for the non-English words. For example, the letter a'yn(ع) is denoted with an apostrophe '. The elongation letters are mostly not reflected in the transliteration. The purpose of this simplification is hopefully to ensure easiness for the unfamiliar reader of the English as opposed to the familiar readers of the language in the world of widely academic transliteration protocols. The superscripts with parenthesis refer to the relevant citations and the superscripts without parenthesis refer to footnotes. In this book, at least one verse from each chapter of the Quran is selected to introduce especially the unfamiliar English reader to the main sacred text of Islam. Instead of using original chapter names as presented above, the selected themes of the verses were carried in the titles for each chapter accompanied with the chapter numbers. The first number in the brackets denotes the above chapter numbers and the second number denotes the verse numbers within the chapter.

1. The Opening

The first chapter of the Quran "al-Fatiha" is often translated as the "opening." It can mean the opening of the meanings or the door of the Quran. The message of the entire Quran is embedded in this short seven-line chapter according to the exegetical scholars. The in-door opening represents knowing one's internal potential self with the teachings of the Quran. The outdoor opening represents knowing the world and universe with the teachings of the Quran.

The Opening

> *In the name of Allah, the All Merciful, the Very Merciful*

All praise and all appreciation belongs to *Allah.*

Allah, Rabb, the Originator, the Upholder and the Maintainer[44] of all
the universes, heavens and galaxies,[45]

Allah, the All Merciful, the Very Merciful

Allah, the only Authority and Decision-Maker of the Day of
Accountability.

---

44. Rabb is translated as Allah with the Arabic context of the Originator, Upholder, and Maintainer in this context. The classical translations [5][6][4][3][2][7] for Rabb in other texts come generally with the word "Lord" except the M. Asad's translation [1]. Language is a constant changing phenomena with time, context, and culture. A word a decade ago may not have the same contextual meaning when used today in our time. The word Lord in classical English can refer to the authority and ownership with slavery with negative embedded meanings [8] in our current time. Also, especially in Christian theology, the word "Lord" commonly used for Jesus which may cause confusion for the reader. One of the common words in daily usage of this word today, is related to the owner of a property referred as landlord. This popular usage can impose some reductive meanings for the general English reader for this word. Oppositely, in Arabic, Rabb has many meanings such as upbringing, nourishing, teaching, making order, upkeeping, caregiving, controlling, safeguarding, and maintaining with love, mercy, and care. Therefore, the best example of the usage of this word in Arabic can be that when parents have a relationship with their child with all these qualities of the word Rabb with love, mercy, and care. In this text, different attributes and names of Allah are embedded in the contextual meanings of Rabb. One can realize the similar approach in M. Asad's translation [1]. He uses Sustainer as the translation of Rabb, which is a very good attempt to change the traditional vocabulary for this word, but I think it is not sufficient to include all the meanings of Rabb depending on the context.

45. Alamin is translated as the galaxies which are observable and predictable in astrophysics. The word galaxy is also known and is commonly used. In this text, specific technical and scientific terminologies are avoided if they are not known and used in the everyday language of English. Universe and heaven are inserted to reflect the classical translations for the word of Alamin.

Allah, You alone, we do worship, and
Allah, from You alone, we do seek help.

Oh *Allah,* guide us to the continuous permanent correct and straight
    path
Oh *Allah,* to the path of those on whom You have showered Your
    Grace and Blessings,
Oh *Allah,* not to the path of those who claim to follow Your guidelines
    but are disrespectful of You,
Oh *Allah,* not to the path of those who claim to love You but don't
    follow the true guidelines from You,

Amen.
[1:1–7]

Commentary

The name of this chapter is called the Opening. This is the first chapter
of the Quran, short in length but dense in meaning according to the
scholars. Therefore, this chapter is critical in practice. It is repeated every
day in the prayers. Some of the scholars think that this short chapter
has the essential meaning of the Quran. In the narrations, there was a
person who was sick during the time of early followers. A friend of the
Prophet read this seven-line chapter to the sick and blew on his body
and the person was cured. The incident was reported to the Prophet.
The Prophet smiled and said "The chapter of Opening is a cure."[10]

Some of the scholars explain that Allah سبحانه وتعالى is teaching us how
to pray to Allah سبحانه وتعالى in this short chapter as well. The first four
lines explain who Allah سبحانه وتعالى is. The second two lines explain
the person's mental and spiritual position in prayer. The last four lines
are the prayer itself. In other words, in the first lines, Allah سبحانه وتعالى
explains the Divine Self. In the second part, the person places his or her
position in the relationship with Allah سبحانه وتعالى, and then finally, the
person asks from Allah سبحانه وتعالى about one's most important needs
in a very condensed form in everyday life.[41]

Discussion Questions

1.   Why does the Quran start with this chapter?
2.   Why is this chapter read repetitively in daily prayers?

2.   This Book

This Book

Alef. Laaaam. Meeeem.[46]

Here[47] is the Noble Book for you,
There is no doubt in it
This Book is Precise, Distinct, True, Real, Clear, Strong, Evident, and
Pure
Guidance for *the ones*
who have the attitude of humbleness, love, sincerity and respect for
Allah[48]
The ones who believe in the unseen and mysterious realities beyond the
senses as revealed from Allah[49]
The ones who regularly establish and engage in prayers: physically,
mentally, and spiritually[50]
The ones who spend and share what We have given to them from:
wealth, knowledge, and kindness
The ones who believe in the Quran, the Bible: Gospel, Psalms, the
Torah, and any prior Books from Allah[51]

---

46. These are the three names of letters in Arabic sounding as A, L, and M in English. No one knows what it means except Allah according to the exegetical scholars. Although there are some discussions about the possible meanings of these letters, Allah starts the scripture with some unknown codes to teach humans the attitude of humbleness that there are limits of human knowledge and mind but humility, acceptance, and respect are the key elements in learning and practice.
47. Zalika in Arabic is composed of three letters, "za, lam, and kaf." The word "here" to indicate nearness for the letter "za"; noble indicating distance and highness for the letter "lam"; and the letter "kaf" indicating "a personal book, for you" with the pronoun "ka." Other translations use the word "that" to translate this word to imply respect for far distance which is in Arabic but English does not carry this meaning with the word "that."
48. Muttaqin is translated as the attitude of humbleness, love, sincerity and respect for Allah.
49. Al-Ghayb is not present which is the unseen and mysterious realities beyond the senses as revealed from Allah. These are the realities that are beyond the senses and the scope of intellect.
50. Iqama is a word interpreted when used with salah as to be fully concentrated and engaged in the prayer. The expression "regularly establish and engage prayers" is interpreted as minimum requirement of five times daily prayers.
51. For the translation of "unzila ilayka wa min qablika" the normative exegetical interpreted meanings are used.

The ones who believe[52] in the afterlife and the meeting day with Allah with firm conviction

These are the ones who are on the *Guidance* from their Merciful and Nourishing Rabb,[53] and
These are the ones who for sure will be happy, successful and peaceful.[54]
[2:1–5]

Commentary

The first five verses of the second chapter are important to introduce the brief summary of this scripture, the Quran. It first starts with an opening, explaining who can benefit from this book.[55] The line especially emphasizes the people with taqwa who can benefit most from this scripture. Taqwa can be translated as love, fear, and respect of Allah سبحانه وتعالى. A person of taqwa has the sincere intention of learning and improving oneself. According to the many exegetical[56] scholars, the Reminder, the Quran, has four main themes: understanding the notion of believing in one Creator; establishing the justice and ethical behavior; rationalizing the certainty about afterlife, accountability, and meeting with Allah سبحانه وتعالى; and finally recognizing all these through different means such as the prophets, messengers, and the scriptures. These five verses have these four themes embedded in their meanings.

Discussion Questions
1. What is the meaning of Alef. Laaaam. Meeeem?
2. Why does the Quran require believing in the Bible: the Gospel, the Psalms, and the Torah, not only the Quran itself?
3. Why is there an adjective "with certainty" for the belief of the afterlife but none in other types of beliefs?

---

52. Muqinun is translated as the belief with rational firm conviction due to the word "iyqaan."
53. Rabb is translated as the Merciful and the Nourisher according to the context.
54. Muflihun is translated as happy, successful, and peaceful.
55. Hudan lil muttaqin.
56. Exegetical is tafsir in Ar.

Allah[57]

Allah, there is no deity except Allah,
Allah, the Alive and the Active
Allah, the Permanent and the Forever

Sleep or unawareness does not touch *Allah*

Everything on the galaxies[58] belongs to *Allah*
Everything on the earth belongs to *Allah*

Who can claim any power next to *Allah*?
except if Allah gives permission

Allah knows everything
secret or public,
internal or external,
past or future.

Who can get anything from *Allah's* knowledge?
except if Allah gives permission
Allah's control[59] surrounds and overpowers everything
the galaxies and the earth.
Who can maintain and uphold their complicated structure in order?[60]
except *Allah*

After all this, understand!
Allah is the Magnificent, the Greatest.
[2:255]

---

57. Ayatal Kursi, literally translates as the Throne verse.
58. In the present discoveries of science, galaxies are the biggest human estimated and observable entities that is used in everyday language. Therefore, the word galaxies is preferred as the closest translation for assamawat.
59. Al-Kursi is translated exegetically as the control, dominion, and authority.
60. Hifz is protection, maintenance, and continuity so that there is no chaos and destruction.

Commentary

This is a very critical verse in the Muslim practice. It is the practice of the Prophet to recite this verse after completing each regular daily prayers. This verse has a distinction in practice because it explains about Allah سبحانه وتعالى. Any verse that directly explains about Allah وتعالى سبحانه has a distinct value.

In everyday practice, people especially read this verse for protection purposes. In a famous narration, the Prophet mentions that if a person reads this verse before sleeping, Allah سبحانه وتعالى sends an angel for that person standing outside his door as a guardian to protect her or him until the person wakes up.[26][10]

Discussion Questions

1. Why is specifically "sleeping" or unawareness mentioned as one of the wrong human constructions about Allah سبحانه وتعالى؟
2. Is tiredness linked with sleeping? How one can understand this in understanding our relationship with Allah سبحانه وتعالى؟ Is it an alienating or non-isolating image of Allah سبحانه وتعالى؟ Why?

The Friend and the Friend

Allah is the *Friend*[61]
of all believers, recognizers appreciators, and grateful ones
Takes them from the depths of piles of darkness, torture and suffering
To the light, peace, joy, and happiness in this life and after death
all other glorified things[62] except Allah are *the friends*
of unrecognizers and unappreciators
Take them from light to the spiritual darkness,[63] torture, stress and
    suffering in this life

---

61. Waliyy is translated as the Friend.
62. Tagut is translated as any deity except Allah. A person's tagut can be anything that person is scared of, or take refuge in, or do an action to please to, except Allah.
63. In the scripture, darkness is plural which implies different depressive states of human psychology and spirituality according to exegetical scholars.

Then, they become the *friends*[64] of torture and suffering[65] after death
Staying there too long[66]...
[2:257]

Commentary

In Islam, pure belief and reliance to one and only Allah سبحانه وتعالى
is the key. Therefore, friends that may imply any type of reliance other
than Allah سبحانه وتعالى can be painful and a problem. Loving the friends
only for the sake of Allah سبحانه وتعالى is important. Loving anything for
Allah سبحانه وتعالى is the key and highest level of relationship with the
creation. The real Friend is always Allah سبحانه وتعالى.

Discussion Questions

1. Who is the real Friend according to the Quran?
2. How can the other friends except Allah سبحانه وتعالى take the
    person to darkness?

Everyone

The prophet believed in the *Revelation*
The believers believed in the *Revelation*

Everyone believed in Allah
Everyone believed in Gabriel, Michael, and all angels
Everyone believed in Bible: the Gospel, the Psalms, and the Torah, and
    Quran and all the books
Everyone believed in Moses, Jesus, Muhammad as the chosen
    messengers from Allah
Everyone believed other messengers and all the prophets chosen by
    Allah
There is *no superiority* of one book over another

---

64. Ashab is translated as the friend.
65. Nar is translated as torture and suffering.
66. Khalidina fiha is translated as staying there too long as one of the minority exegetical
interpretations. This choice also optimize the flow and context. The majority of the translations
render this expression as "staying there infinitely" due to the majority stance of exegetical
interpretations.

There is *no superiority* of one prophet over another
And they ended their proclamation as:
>   We heard and received the message
>   We surrendered and submitted ourselves
>   We ask for Your Forgiveness
>   Oh Our Merciful Rabb!
>   The return is to You
[2:285]

Commentary

This verse outlines the pillars of the Muslim belief system. Islam is not a new religion but continuation of the same message of the Gospel revealed to Prophet Jesus, the same message of Torah revealed to Prophet Moses (PBUH), and the same message of the Quran revealed to Rasulullah ﷺ. In Islamic creed, for example, if a Muslim says "I don't believe in Jesus or Moses (PBUH)," or "I don't believe in the Bible or Torah," then this person is not considered a Muslim in Islamic theology. To remember this creed, the Rasulullah ﷺ recommends every Muslim after the night prayer before going to sleep, reading this verse as a reminder and renewal of their inclusive belief.[10]

Discussion Questions

1.   Why are these verses important in Islamic theology?
2.   Why is it required to believe in the Bible: the Gospel, the Psalms, and the Torah for Muslims?
3.   Why is it required to believe in the teachings of Jesus, Moses (PBUH), and other prophets/messengers sent by Allah سبحانه وتعالى؟
4.   How is the recitation of these verses practiced in daily life in different Muslim societies?

3.   Common Word

Family of Jesus

Alef. Laaaam. Meeeem.

Allah, there is no deity except Allah,
Allah, the Alive and the Active
Allah, the Permanent and the Forever

Allah revealed the Book to you
with the truth, certainty and precision
confirming what Allah already revealed before
The Bible: the Gospel, the Psalms, and the Torah
[3:1–3]

Discussion Question

   1.   What is the position of the Quran compared to other scriptures?

Adam and Jesus

With certainty,
The nature of Jesus to Allah is similar to the nature of Adam
Whom Allah created Adam from dust and
said: "Be", he was.

The truth is from your Teaching and Upbringing Allah. Then,
Don't be from the ones who is hesitant and doubtful.
[3:59–60]

Discussion Questions

   1.   How is the creation of Adam (PBUH) and Jesus similar in theology?
   2.   How is the understanding of Jesus in Islam?
   3.   Why is there an assurance not to doubt in the above verse?

Common Word

Inform all Christians and Jews and other followers of a scripture about
    this amazing fact!

Please pay attention followers of the earlier revelations!

Let's get together and realize the values that you and we hold in
    common!

Among these values, primarily, is:

We worship only to Allah. We should not worship anything except our
    same and common Creator.[67]

This is because; we should not ascribe any equal with Allah.

And therefore, we should not consider human beings as divine.

We believe that only Allah is divine.

After all, if they reject this message then tell them:

"Be our witness that we submit ourselves to one Allah"

[3:64]

Discussion Questions

1. How is the understanding of "common" according to the verse
    above?
2. What is the importance of this verse for different interfaith
    engagements for Muslims, especially in the West?

---

67. The Arabic reader will note that "That we only worship Allah" is inserted in the translation
to give an exegetical complementary meaning to the following part: "We should not worship
anything except to our Same and Common Creator."

Rotation of Days

If an evil touched you
Then remember that
Evil touches others as well.

These are the days
We rotate among the people
The days of good and evil
So that the real characters
Of people are revealed
Allah knows it and
You will be a witness to it as well

Remember!
Allah does not like oppressors
[3:140]

Discussion Questions

1. How can one understand the "rotation of days" among people?
2. Is it possible to avoid evil and live a life without it? What is the importance of prayer to avoid evil in Islam?

4. Creation in Pairs

Creation in Pairs

Oh People!
Have love, conscience, fear, and respect of Your Rabb
Who created you from one self and
Created from this self its pair
And spread you on earth as
Men and women

Have love, conscience, fear, and respect of Your Rabb
From Who you always ask your needs.

Have love, conscience, fear, and respect of Allah
Refrain cutting relationships with each other and with your relatives

Remember!
Indeed, Allah is constantly watching over you.
[4:1].

Commentary

This verse reminds us of the notion of humans as one species, and we are from the same family. Therefore, one should maintain justice and ethical behavior in this understanding of universal brotherhood and sisterhood. It reminds us to have fear and respect for Allah سبحانه وتعالى in order not to go over limits and oppress one another; although people may not realize it but Allah سبحانه وتعالى knows it and there will be accountability after death for each person.

Discussion Question

1.   Why are fear and respect for Allah سبحانه وتعالى repeated in the same verse?

Does Allah oppress?

Indeed and Definitely,
Allah does not oppress even a little
Even of a size or smaller than an atom.

And, oppositely,
If the person has a small good effort,
Allah increases its reward in multitude and
Gives this person special and enormous gifts
From the Grace of the Divine.
[4:40]

Discussion Questions

1.   What is the relationship between authority and oppression?
2.   What are some narratives in our contemporary time for different
     religions about the concept of authority, Allah سبحانه وتعالى, and
     oppression?
3.   Accordingly, how do you understand this verse?
4.   What is the main theological teaching embedded in this verse
     when Allah سبحانه وتعالى gives everyone a multitude of rewards
     for their small, good effort compared to the evil acts that there
     is no increase in the punishment?

Pure Belief

Indeed,
Allah does not forgive a person
if they did not recognize One and Pure Creator before they die,
     making shirk

Other than that,
With the Divine will,
Allah can forgive everyone for all the other wrongs and evil.
[4:48]

Whoever makes shirk, ascribes a partner to Allah, commits a terrible
     sin.

Discussion Question

1. Why is unrecognition of One and Pure Creator not forgiven by Allah سبحانه وتعالى according to the theology but everything else can be forgiven with Allah سبحانه وتعالى's mercy?

Don't they think about this Quran!

After all this,
Don't they critically think about this Quran!
If it was from anyone other than Allah
Definitely, they would find a lot of contradictions in it.
[4:82]

Discussion Questions

1. How can one establish authenticity of a text with critical thinking?
2. What do the above verses urge the readers while engaged in reading the Quran?

The Etiquette of Greeting

And,
If you are greeted with kind words
Then, greet this person better than her or his greeting

Or,
At least, return the same greeting in the similar way of niceness

Indeed, and definitely remember that,
Allah accounts for everything.
[4:86]

Discussion Question

1. Why is greeting a person emphasized and important in theology both in the teachings of the scripture and the Rasulullah ﷺ?

More Truthful Words

There is no deity except Allah
Definitely, Allah will gather you in the Day of Accountability
There is no doubt about it.

Whose words can be more truthful other than Allah's?
[4:87]

Discussion Question

1. Why does Allah سبحانه وتعالى put an emphasis in the scripture about the truthfulness of the Divine words?

Hiding from Who?

They want to hide from people
And
They don't want to hide from Allah
but they cannot hide from Allah

But
Allah is with them
When they are planning the evil
Engaging in conversations
Which Allah is not pleased of it.

Don't worry!
Allah surrounds them
With the Divine Knowledge and Power
[4:108]

Discussion Question

1. Can one stop doing an evil alone if he or she knows that one is being watched by Allah سبحانه وتعالى؟ Why?

5.   Conflict and Justice

Conflict and Justice

Oh you who believe!
Be the ones who are consistent witnesses
In establishing the justice for the sake of Allah
And don't let the hate or dislike of a group
Deviate you from justice

Be just and fair!
This the closest character of a person who is Allah conscious
Fear and have respect for Allah!
Allah knows what you are doing.
[5:8]

Discussion Question

1. According to the verse above, how is the relationship between fairness of a person and one's closeness to Allah سبحانه وتعالى in piety?

The Prophet, the Quran, and the Followers of the Bible: the Gospel, the Psalms, and the Torah and the Educated People

Oh Educated People![68], Christians, and Jews who follow the Bible: the
       Gospel, the Psalms, and the Torah!
Indeed, Our Messenger came to you
Explaining to you what you have been much hiding from the books,
       the Bible: the Gospel, the Psalms, and the Torah
Overlooking to your mistakes much
Without any blame and exposure of your mistakes much

---

68. Ahlu Kitab is translated with the classical exegetical meanings and with a contemporary meaning of a person who may have an education represented with the notions of learning from the books.

Oh Educated People, Christians, and Jews who follow the Bible: the
Gospel, the Psalms, and the Torah!
Indeed,
a light, Rasulullah 🕌 and
a clear book, the Quran
has come to you from Allah.

Allah guides with this Prophet and this Book to the Divine pleasure
and to the path of peace
Taking them out from the ocean of darkness to the light and peace
with the will of Allah and
Guiding them to a continuous and permanent correct and peaceful life.
[5:15–16].

Discussion Questions

1. Why do all the prophets such as Rasulullah 🕌, Moses (PBUH),
    Jesus, or others always come complementing each other with
    similar teachings according to Islamic theology?
2. How is the position of the Rasulullah 🕌 for the followers of
    Christianity and Judaism?

6.   Ecosystem and Species

Knowing about the Prophet with Certainty

The ones who we gave them scripture such as the Bible: the Gospel, the
    Psalms, and the Torah
Know and recognize the Rasulullah ﷺ
As if they recognize and know their own children with certainty.
After this,
If they deny this fact, they betray their own moral values
Then,
The ones who betray their own selves are not going to believe.
[6:20]

Discussion Question

1. Why are Christians, Jews, and other Divine bookholders
    expected to know and recognize the Rasulullah ﷺ with
    certainty?

Lying against Their Own Selves

Look at those!
How they lie against their own selves and
Whatever they are making up
Will leave them alone
[6:24]

Discussion Question

1. What is meant by "they lie against their own selves"?

Ecosystem and Species

There is no moving creature on the earth or
Flying with wings in the sky except that

They are communities and species like yours, humans, in the
        ecosystem.

We have not left out anything in the book
Then, ultimately, they will be returned and gathered to their Rabb,
        Allah
[6:38]

Discussion Question

   1.   How does this theology teach all moving creatures to have their
        community?

Appreciating the Scriptures Revealed by Allah

They did not appreciate Allah with a true appreciation[69] when they
        said:
Allah did not reveal anything to any human being
Then, ask them:
Who revealed the book, the Torah, that came to Moses?
And this book was a clear light and guidance for the people.

[and] which you treat as [mere] leaves of paper, disclosing [some of it]
        while hiding most of it

---

69. This appreciation can change depending on the societies and time. For example, the
initial Meccan pagans did know Allah but at the same time they worshipped other idols.
This was not the true appreciation of Allah. The people of the scriptures such as Christians or
Jews had changes in the original teachings of their creed and theology that were brought
by their messengers/prophets such as Jesus or Moses (PBUH). Some of them followed these
false teachings. This was not the true appreciation of Allah. The Muslims had the authentic
teachings of Allah with the Quran and with the teachings of the Rasulullah 🕊. Yet, some of
them did not apply these teachings fully in their practice. This was not the true appreciation
of Allah.

On the other hand,
You were taught about a knowledge
Neither you nor your fathers[70] knew before.

If still they don't accept it.
Just tell them:
Definitely, Allah revealed this
If still they don't accept it, then
Leave them in their own occupation in a self-deceptive game.
[6:91]

Discussion Question

1. What is the position of the Quran compared to the Bible: the Gospel, the Psalms, and the Torah in Islam?

---

70. Fathers can denote the knowledge transferred from cultures.

7.   Doing the evil and blaming others?

Doing the evil and blaming others?

And when they do evil they say:
"Indeed, we have inherited this act from our culture[71] and society
And also, Allah ordered us to do this."
Tell them:
Definitely, Allah does not order doing any evil!
Are you making up something about Allah that really you don't know?

Tell them:
My Upbringing and Just, Rabb, Allah always orders the good, the
     ethical, the fair and the just.
And , that pray and turn to Allah in all places of worship and
     prostration
Call Allah with sincerity, only believing and trusting in One!
That is the due of the religion only for Allah
And remember!
As you were nothing, you were created in the beginning
You will return to Allah at the end.
[7:28–29]

Discussion Questions

1. How is the psychology of blaming others when there is an evil?
2. Why do people blindly follow or not follow a culture or social
     norms?
3. How do you compare following a religion or a belief in a culture
     compared to ethical values? Are they similar or different? Why?

---

71. Abaana is translated as "culture and society" instead of forefathers or fathers as translated in other translations. Current, more popular usage of inheriting a habit and doing it as a norm is named as culture and social values as Tylor state**s**. (*Popular Science Monthly* 26 (1884): 145. Public Domain.)

8.   Uniting the Hearts

© PiXXart/Shutterstock.com

Uniting the Hearts

And,
Allah united their hearts.
If you spent all the wealth and resources on the earth
You were not able to unite their hearts.
But only Allah united them.
Definitely, Allah is the High, the Exalted, and the Source of Wisdom
    and Authority.
[8:63]

Discussion Question

1. How can a person use the above teaching in one's life when
    there is a conflict?

9.   Trade

Trade

Allah bought from the believers their lives, body, and wealth
With the repayment of Heaven.
[9:111]

Commentary

Body, health, time, physical and mindful strength are advanced payments for the person to use and invest in good given by Allah سبحانه وتعالى according to Islam. Therefore, the body, the lifetime, health, opportunities, strength, wealth, and mind are all tools to use in this investment.

Although the person does not really own him or herself, it is granted by Allah سبحانه وتعالى on the earth as a trust [33:72] as if the person has the full ownership and control over oneself. This is due to the Allah سبحانه وتعالى-given free will of the person.

It is expected to make good investments with these tools. These investments are not forced but the person has the free will to choose evil or good. Therefore, in the Quran, this notion of business with Allah سبحانه وتعالى is presented. Islamic teachings encourage the middle way in both worldly and spiritual matters as the person has bodily and spiritual needs.

Discussion Question

1.   How is the relationship between the person and Allah سبحانه وتعالى symbolized as a trade in the above verse?

Categories

Give good news to the believers!
The ones *who try to always* seek repentance from *Allah*
The ones who try to always worship *Allah*
The ones who try to always be grateful to *Allah*
The ones who try to always travel for the sake of *Allah*
The ones who try to always bow and prostrate to Allah in their prayer
The ones who try to always encourage the good and prevent the evil and
     bad things
The ones who try to always observe the limits set by *Allah*.
[9:112]

Discussion Question

1. How do you understand different categorization of people in
    their relationship with Allah?

10.   Are you going to force people to believe?

Are you going to force people to believe?

And
If your Merciful, Just, and Caregiving Rabb wanted
Definitely, everyone on the earth will believe in Allah
After this,
Are you going to force people to believe in Allah?
[10:99]

Discussion Questions

1. Is belief a choice in theology? How and why?
2. Does the Quran teach forcing people to believe?
3. How can one explain the narratives about "forced conversions" of the expansion of Islam in some of the historical narratives?

Alternation of Night and Day

Surely, in the alternation of night and day and
In what Allah has created in the skies, galaxies and the universe and
     the earth,
There are signs for people who are Conscious of Allah.

As for those who do not believe in meeting with Us and
are quite happy with the life of this world and
are content with it,
then those are the ones who are neglectful of Our signs.
[10:6–7]

Discussion Question

1. What is a sign according to the Quran?

11.   Continuous Struggle

Continuous Struggle

After all this,
Struggle constantly
To be on the straight and correct path
As you are instructed
With the ones who turn to Allah

Do not oppress and pass the limits!

Definitely and Surely,
Allah sees and is aware of
With what you are constantly preoccupied.
[11:112]

Discussion Questions

1.   Is it difficult to constantly struggle for spiritual cleansing? Why?
2.   What is important for theology: the effort of struggle or the ultimate result of the struggle as failure or achievement? Why?

12.   Language of the Revelation

© samiph222/Shutterstock.com

The first verse and the first word revealed to the Rasulullah ﷺ from Allah سبحانه وتعالى was to "Read." It meant to read, learn, and think about all the signs of Allah سبحانه وتعالى. The verse is written in Arabic in a style of calligraphy.

Language of the Revelation

Alif. Laaaam. Raa.

These are the verses of the clear Book.

For sure and definitely,
We revealed the Quran
In the language of Arabic,
So that there is no confusion
of originality and authenticity
That you can use your mind and intellect.[72]
[12:1–2]

Discussion Question

1.   Why is the language of the revelation as Arabic specifically mentioned in the Quran itself?

---

72. Arabic language has a mathematical structure. A person can derive other words from the same word if one knows the rules of derivation. Therefore, non-Arabs can learn this language at any age easily and even speak without an accent with proper eloquent Arabic better than a native speaker. It is interesting to note that only 10% (~200 million) of the Muslim population is native Arabs and the rest are non-Arabs (~1.8 billion).

The Best Story

We tell you
The best story of all
From what we have revealed
In this Quran,

And, indeed,
You were not informed,
Before.
[12:3]

Commentary

The best story mentioned above is the story of Joseph (PBUH), the son of Jacob (PBUH), mentioned in detail in the Quran. The story has a variety of appeals, motifs, and themes: linguistic eloquence of the full story, notions of wisdom, patience, unexpected events, always reliance on Allah سبحانه وتعالى, and opportunistic theories. One can interestingly relate this to the contemporary themes of the movie-making industry with the notions of power (position), love, religion, imprisonment, parents, jealousy, hatred, women, game theory, and dreams. It is interesting to note also that a lot of people who became Muslim tend to choose the name of Joseph (PBUH) (Yusuf) due to this story explained in the Quran.

Discussion Question

1.   Why is this story deemed to be the best in the Quran?

13.   Moving the Mountains, Cracking the Earth, and Speaking with the Dead

© maxicam/Shutterstock.com

Moving the Mountains, Cracking the Earth, and Talking with Dead

If there is a book that
could move mountains,
destroy the earth, or
compel the dead to speak

Then, definitely it would have been
This Book, the Quran.
[13:31]

Discussion Questions

1.   What makes the Quran so important in theology and practice?
2.   What are some possible talismanic usages of the Quran in practice?

14.   A Nice Word and a Nice Tree

A Simple Good Word and a Nice, Strong Tree

Don't you see
How Allah brings the example
Of a simple simple, good and pleasant
Similar to a nice tree:

Its roots are very strong and
Its branches are in the sky.
[14:24]

Discussion Questions

1. How can a good word be similar to a nice tree?
2. What is the relationship of the root of the tree being strong and branches in the sky and a good word?

15.   Upgraded and Downgraded

I Wish

Alif. Laaaam. Ra.
These are the verses of the Book,
The clear Quran.

Many will wish from the ungrateful ones,
I wish I had followed the true way of God- the way of peace.[73]
[15:1–2]

Discussion Question

1.   Why is the importance of following the true and correct way of
     Allah سبحانه وتعالى in the Quran emphasized so much?

Upgraded and Downgraded

We know who is upgraded constantly
We know who is downgraded constantly
[15:24]

Commentary

There is a notion of daily struggle in advancing the spiritual relationship
on the path of Allah سبحانه وتعالى. One can make a resemblance of the
bull and bear markets in the stock market, for example. A prime example
of the downgrade is Satan when he was at the highest level then he
becomes at the lowest in his closeness to Allah سبحانه وتعالى. Therefore,
in practice, as long as the person is alive, the person can spiritually
excel or lose depending on the struggle, intention, and sincerity. No
one knows their true spiritual state until the person meets with Allah
سبحانه وتعالى. Although the time of death is unknown, a sinner can
become very pious and a pious person can become an evil person in

---

73. Muslim is translated as not as a group phenomenon but means following "true way of
Allah." The same word is used for Abraham (PBUH) as a Muslim although he was historically
long before the religion of Islam.

their journey of life before they die. The spiritual state of the person right before death is very critical because the person will meet Allah سبحانه وتعالى in this state. According to this theology, this final spiritual state of the person will determine the final and permanent abode of the person in the Afterlife. Due to the uncertainty of the time of death for each person, each person is expected to be watchful of their morals and levels of piety regarding people, and Allah سبحانه وتعالى.

Discussion Question

1. How can the uncertainty of gaining or losing on the spiritual path affect a person in their struggle?

16.   The Bee

**The Quranic verses suggest that we should think and
reflect on different beings to realize the perfection of how
Allah creates and inspires and teaches even
the animals in their complicated engagements**

Milk, Blood, and Excretion

And, for sure, there is a lesson for you in cattle, sheep, goats….
We feed you from their bellies.
A pure and pleasant milk comes miraculously
From a place between
Blood and excretion meet.
[16:66]

Bee

And,
your Merciful, Upbringing, and Caregiving Rabb inspired to the bee
to take homes on mountains, trees, and hives.
[16:68]

Commentary

The Quran constantly urges the reader to think about different beings
on the earth and how they benefit the humans.

1. How can one view daily routines or incidents as something normal or abnormal?
2. What are the two different approaches or questions that religion, Islam, and science are seeking to answer for the living and non-living things? Are science and religion complementary in Islam?

Things Other Than Allah

And,
What they worship other than Allah,
Cannot create anything.
They are themselves created.
[16:20]

Discussion Question

1. Why does the Quran constantly emphasize to challenge the deities if they have the ability of creating and giving life to something?

Two gods?

And Allah said:
Don't adopt two gods,
Don't adopt two deities, or
Don't adopt anything that is overpowering you other than Allah
For sure, your Creator, Allah is only One.

Therefore, to Me alone, stand in awe!
[16:51]

Commentary

In external affairs or laws of theology, the Creator of everything is Allah سبحانه وتعالى: Good and bad, ugly and beautiful, Satan and angels... Every creation has a purpose. Allah سبحانه وتعالى allows a similar free market of good and evil to potentially let the humans use their free will in decision-making. It does not mean that Allah سبحانه وتعالى is passive, created and left everything, and everything is on their own now. Rather, there is a continuous intervention and creation of Allah سبحانه وتعالى in nature. In a person's life, Allah سبحانه وتعالى's intervention can be very obvious and clear for some people, and for some, it can be mystical and especially based on wisdom.

There is no duality in understanding who the Creator is. Allah سبحانه وتعالى is only One. In external guidelines of theology, although a person can verbally accept this notion of surrendering oneself to One and only Allah سبحانه وتعالى, in practice, a spiritual journey exists to perfect the understanding of this notion internally. In other words, if a person is scared of anything other than Allah سبحانه وتعالى, this perspective of duality of two deities still can exist. The goal of a spiritual purification is to struggle lifelong in order to turn fully to only one Allah سبحانه وتعالى alone.

Discussion Questions

1. Is it easy or difficult to discharge oneself from all worries except Allah سبحانه وتعالى? Why?
2. How can it help the person if the person does not have any real worries except the relationship with Allah سبحانه وتعالى?

Ethical Behavior

Certainly,
Allah orders justice, fairness, and
Niceness, good conduct, and
Generosity towards one's fellow-men.

And forbids
Immorality and unethical behavior,
Evil,
Oppression.

Allah is giving you advice.

So that, perhaps, you indeed take this advice and think about it.
[16:90]

Discussion Questions

1. According to the above verse, what is good and evil?
2. What is the significance of the above verse in Friday sermons for Muslims?

17. Beautiful Names of Allah

Doing Good

If you do good it is for your own benefit
If you do something bad it is against your own self
[17:7]

Discussion Questions

1. How is this verse understood in practice?
2. Is the understanding of "karma" similar to the teaching of this verse?

Calling Evil as Good

And the person calls and wants the evil
As if he or she calls and wants the good
The nature of the human is always hasty
[17:11]

Discussion Question

1. How can a person want the evil assuming that it is good?

The Levels of People

Look!
How we make some people above others
Remember!
The levels in the afterlife will be better and higher than this!
[17:21]

Discussion Questions

1. Are the levels in the above verse related to the spiritual or worldly levels?
2. Are the levels in this world related to the levels in the afterlife? For example, if someone is rich, is this person considered blessed or spiritually higher than a poor person according to Islam?

Chanting and Glorification of Allah by All the Beings

All the seven skies and galaxies and earth and between them
Praise, glorify and chant for Allah

There is nothing left out from all the beings except they perform
The Praise, glorification and chant for their Merciful Creator

But you don't understand their chants
Remember your Allah is always Caring, Gentle and Forgiving.
[17:44]

Discussion Question

1.   Are there people who understand and hear the glorifications of
     other beings?

The Character of the Person

And when we give something good to the person
This person turns away from Allah and does not care.

When an evil hits this person
She or he becomes hopeless

Tell them:
Everyone shows and acts according to their own character
Therefore, your Watchful and Merciful Rabb knows who is better on
      the path.
[17:83,84]

Discussion Question

1.   Do the humans naturally tend to appreciate good? Why?

Challenge to All Creation about the Quran

Tell this challenge to them:
If all the humans and Jinns (other beings)[74] come together
To put together a Quran similar to this one
For sure, they will not be able to bring a similar one
Even if they support each other fully on this task
[17:88]

Discussion Questions

1. How is this challenge understood in practice? What is the essence of this challenge?
2. How can the order "tell them" be interpreted in the above verse? Who is giving this order?

What prevents a person from believing and accepting?

People being prevented from believing
When the guidance come to them is only due to
Their statement:
"Does Allah send a human as a messenger?"

Tell them:
If on the earth lived angels instead of humans
Then, we would send them an angel as a messenger

Therefore, tell them:
Allah is sufficient as a witness between me and you
Indeed, Allah is always the Knower and the Seer of the true state
Of all Allah's creation
[17:94–97]

Discussion Questions

1. Why do the humans expect a non-human messenger from Allah سبحانه وتعالى? What is their reason or rationale?
2. How is the response to this expectation in the above verse?

---

74. Jinn is translated as non-humans for the English reader.

The Beautiful Names of Allah

Say:
You call your Creator as Allah or the Most Merciful, Ar-Rahman
It doesn't matter!

Whatever name you call your Merciful Allah with
Definitely, your Creator has all the beautiful names

And when you communicate with your Hearing and Seeing Allah in
    your prayers
You don't need to raise your voice or whisper
Be natural, be in between and follow the middle way
[17:110]

Discussion Questions

1. According to the theology, what is the significance of calling
   and knowing Allah سبحانه وتعالى with the beautiful names?
2. Which one is more important, having knowledge about Allah
   سبحانه وتعالى with correct understanding or referring to Allah
   سبحانه وتعالى with the special or proper names in the scriptures?
   Why?

18.   Appreciating the Book

Arabic Calligraphy of AL HAMDU LILLAHI, which means all true appreciation is for Allah only. There are chapters of the Quran which start with this expression. This chapter starts with the appreciation of and thanking Allah about the revelation of the Quran. This expression is written in Arabic calligraphy in the above picture.

Appreciation for the Book

Thanks and all appreciation to Allah that
Allah revealed the book for the person who recognizes and appreciates
    Allah[75]
And this book does not have any mistake or error in it,
Is fully perfect.
[18:1]

Discussion Questions

1. Why should there be an appreciation when Allah سبحانه وتعالى communicates with the creation through a formal scripture?
2. How can someone's attitude be with the Book who recognizes and appreciates Allah سبحانه وتعالى compared to its opposite?
3. Why is it emphasized that this Book is perfect and there are no errors or mistakes?

---

75. Although, the book is revealed to the Prophet to convey to other humans. The notion of personalization is important in theology as if the scripture is an individual revelation to each person to directly communicate with Allah without any intermediator.

19.   Do you hear anything from the dead?

© Marc Bruxelle/Shutterstock.com

Talking of Baby Jesus in the Cradle

Then, Mary pointed to Jesus.
People said:
How can we talk to a baby in the cradle?
Baby Jesus said:
"I am the servant and creation of Allah.
Allah gave me the Book and
Made me a prophet and messenger."
[19:29–30]

Commentary

According to the above verse, people did not understand how Mary had a baby and they were shocked. Mary at that point reserved her right not to talk, kept silent, but pointed to Jesus. At that time, baby Jesus in the cradle talked as a miracle.

Discussion Questions

1.   How can one understand baby Jesus's talking in the cradle in theology?
2.   How is the understanding of Jesus in Islam according to the above verse?

Do you hear anything from the dead?

And,
We terminated before them many generations.
Do you feel, see or hear even a whisper from the dead or past nations?
[19:98]

Discussion Question

1. What does the above verse imply about the reality of death and communication with death?

20.   Is the Quran for difficulty?

Taha

Ta ha.
We did not reveal the Quran to you
so that you have difficulty
But as a reminder for the one
who is humble
[20:1–3]

Discussion Questions

1. What is the purpose of scriptures?
2. Why does the verse mention the possibility of the following of a scripture being difficult for some people?
3. Why does the verse mention that the Quran was not revealed in order to put the difficulty on the person?
4. How does the state of being humble affect learning?
5. What is the meaning of Taha in popular practice?

21.   The Manual of a Person

The Manual of a Person

For sure and certainly,
We revealed you a book.
Inside, you, yourself is explained
It is talking about you[76]
Don't you understand?
[21:10]

Discussion Question

1.   Is the Quran a manual for a person?

---

76. Addition of a sentence, due to the contextual meaning.

22.   Creation Process

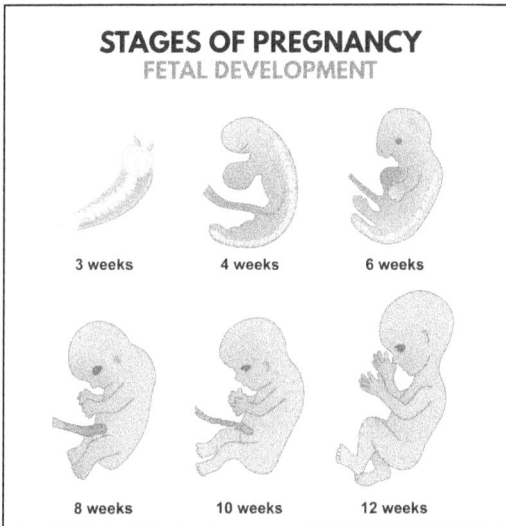

STAGES OF PREGNANCY
FETAL DEVELOPMENT

3 weeks   4 weeks   6 weeks

8 weeks   10 weeks   12 weeks

© Marochkina Anastasiia/Shutterstock.com

Human embryo, stages of fetal development by week

Creation Process

Oh People!
If you have doubt about recreation after death,

Then, remember!

We created you from the elements on the earth.
In a specific process of sperm and an egg
Then, an embryo,
Then, a growing being with its flesh, and bones but still incomplete,

Keep in mind, we are explaining some of the details of the creation
    process

Then, we keep this being dwelling and developing in the womb
Until a designated time We want…

Finally, this being comes out as a baby so that it can gain some power

After all, some of you die early, some die later

So that everyone completes the journey of knowing and experience

Another creation example is from what you see every day in the
        garden, on the earth
It looks like there is no plant, but it is dead.
As soon as we send rain on it
It gets alive, starts growing, and becomes green
Such nice looking flowers, roses, fruits...

After all these examples,

Don't doubt about Allah

Allah is Real and the Truth
Allah creates from nothing
Allah recreates from death
Allah is all Powerful.

There is no doubt,
That the meeting time with Allah is close
Allah will recreate all the death from graves and from anywhere,
        doesn't matter

After all this, don't bring arguments
without any knowledge,
without any education,
without any authentic reference
[22:5–8]

Discussion Questions

   1.   What is the Quranic explanation of the stages of embryonic
        development?
   2.   What can be the reasons that the Quran gives specific details of
        embryonic stages?
   3.   How does the Quran relate the details of embryonic development
        to the recreation after death?

23.   The Purpose

Purpose

Do you think that
You were created for nothing, for no purpose?

And,
Do you think that
You will not be returned to Us?

After this,
Allah is the Ultimate True Authority.
There is no deity except Allah,
Allah is the Merciful Sustaining Rabb and Owner of the Great and
        Noble Authority, Arshul Karim.[77]
[23:115–116]

Discussion Question

  1.   What is the purpose of a human being according to the Quran?

Power struggle?

Then the aristocrats and the upper class of the unappreciators from his
        people said: What is going on!

"This person is a human like you.

He just wants power.

And even,
If really Allah wanted to send a messenger or prophet
Then it would be an angel instead of a human,

---

77. Merciful Sustainer and Owner is for the word Rabb. Please see the discussion about the
translation of the word "Rabb" in Surah Fatiha. Arshul Karim as Great and Noble Authority.

A human messenger is really a weird concept
We haven't heard or seen this type of teaching in our present and
      previous culture, forefathers or society.[78]
[23:24]

Commentary

The above story is a portion mentioning a dialogue of the Prophet Noah (PBUH) to believe in the One and only Creator with his community. The people in that community reject his message and interpret that he wants power.

Discussion Question

1. According to the verse above, what are the reasons for people not to believe in the teaching of the Prophet Noah (PBUH) as mentioned in the Quran?

---

78. Here, "abainaal awwaliin" is translated as "previous culture, forefathers and society" due to contemporary contextualization of this phrase.

24.   Walking on Belly and Feet

Walking on Belly and Feet

And,
Allah created all the moving creatures from water.

Then,
Some move and crawl on their belly and

Some walk on their two feet

Some walk on their four feet.

Allah creates how ever Allah wants.

Definitely and for sure,

Allah has the power to do anything.
[24:45]

Discussion Question

1.   How does the Quran gauge a person to think by mentioning "moving on belly and feet"?

25. Shadow and Change

Shadow and Change

Have you not observed how your All-Knowing and Merciful Rabb
stretched out the shadow (of the sun)?
If Allah so willed, Allah would have made it stand still.
But, We made the sun an indicator for it.
[25:45]

Commentary

The concept of change is mentioned in different contexts in the Quran. Muslims can increase their engagement with the rituals, chanting, or prayers before and after sunset and sunrise. The Quran especially encourages people to engage themselves with remembrance of Allah سبحانه وتعالى through dhikr, chanting, or prayer during the times of sunset and sunrise.

Discussion Questions

1. How can external change affect the spiritual state of heart and mind?
2. How can the shadow of the objects inspire one in the relationship with the Divine?

Arrogance or prostration as a sign of respect?

And they were advised
To prostrate as a sign of respect of Allah, the Most Merciful

They said:
"Who is the Most Merciful?
Do you really think we would respect and prostrate to what you tell us?"

And,
This attitude of arrogance in reality increased their hate.
[25:60]

Commentary

The above verse is recognized as a verse of prostration. There are fourteen occasions of such verses in the Quran. Some of the verses of prostration show the intrinsic qualities of humans for arrogance. When the Prophet read the above verse, he prostrated. Therefore, when Muslims read this verse and some other similar ones they prostate. Prostration can be understood as one's attitude as a sign of respect and humility for Allah سبحانه وتعالى. By doing the act of prostration, they show their physical disagreements with the arrogant ones.

Discussion Question

1. Why do the people give negative responses if they are called to recognize and be respectful to Allah سبحانه وتعالى, the Most Merciful?

26.   The Poets and Magicians

The Poets and Magicians

Ta. Seeen. Meeeem.
These are the verses of a clear Book.
You will almost destroy yourself due to to grief because
They don't appreciate and recognize Allah.

We appreciate your genuine and deep concern but don't Worry!

If We wanted we could have brought to them the signs
Which would have forced them to be humble and appreciative.
And,
When they had a new reminder from the Most Merciful, Allah
Their attitude was only to say "I don't care"

For sure,
They are denying it but
Soon, they will have the news and the results of
What they have been denying, and not caring about.
[26:1–6]

Discussion Questions

1. Does Allah سبحانه وتعالى appreciate and reward the people who
    have concern about others knowing Allah سبحانه وتعالى؟
2. How can one understand the above verses for the responsibility
    of the Rasulullah ﷺ's invitation?

The Poets and Magicians

(Taqi Usmani):
 So they threw down their ropes and their staffs and said, "By the
  majesty of Pharaoh, we will be the triumphant for sure."
 Then Moses (PBUH) threw down his staff, and in no time it started
  swallowing the falsehood they invented.

Jaabir's translation:
 They threw down their ropes and their staffs,
 Saying, "By Pharaoh's Majesty we'll triumph at last."
 And, then Moses (PBUH) threw down his staff,
  and in no time it swallowed the falsehood they had
[26:44]

Commentary

The above verse is an example of how the sounds of the Quran, the selection of words, and the overall meaning portrays the scene. The context of the above verses is about the magicians' use of magic with the tools of ropes and bending long items. These words with different conjugations are underlined and colored above. The selected words in Arabic give this very vivid act of both magicians and the response of Moses (PBUH). The etymological meaning of the words implies the illusional effect of magicians with these tools. In evil effects of magic practiced for thousands of years, most of the time the effect on a person comes with round, string, and rope shaped items and geometries. One can read these verses to use as an antidote for the poison of magic along with other litanies. In practice, it is also accepted that there are the temporary effects of magic and sometimes poems on the person. But the permanent, useful, and peaceful effect is only with the Quran, the practices of the Rasulullah ﷺ, and other original scriptures and litanies according to the Islamic teachings.

Discussion Questions

 1. How can one rationalize the importance of reading a divine scripture from its original language of revelation?
 2. What is the understanding of magic and poetry in Islam?

27.   Allah from the Bird's Eye

Allah from the Bird's Eye

The bird said:

"During my travel,

I have found a queen and her people prostrating and worshipping
themselves to the sun, instead of Allah, and the Satan has falsely
beautified their actions for them, and therefore

prevented them from the right way, so they do not choose the guidance
I really don't understand!

Shouldn't they prostrate and worship Allah who brings forth what is
hidden in the heavens and the earth, and

Shouldn't they prostrate and worship Allah who knows whatever you
hide and whatever you do in public.

Allah! There is no god but Allah, the Merciful Authoritative Rabb of
the Great Authority and Control."[79]

[27:24–26]

Commentary

As mentioned in the previous part of the verse, the bird gets into a very
intellectual and rational argument with the Prophet Soloman (PBUH).
The conversation is about a country that the bird found in its excursion.
From the character of the bird, it shows that the bird has a clear and
definite belief of one Creator. It gives examples in its conversation with
Soloman (PBUH) about the majesty of Allah سبحانه وتعالى and how
Allah سبحانه وتعالى creates. The bird first cannot rationalize the people
worshipping the sun as the Creator as the verse reads as above. Later,
the bird mentions that their irrational belief could be due to Satan's
misguidance. Satan can show something false as true by using different
deceitful beautification or ornamentation methods. Lastly, the bird
engages with a real intense theological argument of understanding the
divinity and the Creator in the Quran.

---

79. Arsh is translated as Great Authority and Control.

Discussion Questions

1. What is the understanding of animals, plants, and objects in their relationship with Allah سبحانه وتعالى in Islam?

2. How does the bird rationalize the understanding of Allah سبحانه وتعالى in the above verse?

28.   Choice of the Religion and Fear of Losing the Wealth

Choosing a Religion and Fear of Losing the Wealth

And they said:
"If we follow the guidance that is with you then
We will be forced to leave our land and belongings"

If that is the case then, then ask them:

Didn't We place them in a secure and safe country
Where all different types of fruits of wealth are pouring
As a favor from Us?

And, but still
Most of them are making excuses and are unaware of this truth
[28:57]

Discussion Questions

1.   What are the factors that prevent people from following a religion even though they may agree with its teachings?
2.   Are we living in a secure and safe country to make our own choices about religion? Why?
3.   Who are the people that are expressing their fear of losing their wealth if they become Muslims in the above verse?

29. Struggle

© PHOTOCREO Michal Bednarek/Shutterstock.com

Trials and Struggle

Alif, Laam, Meem.
Do the people think that they will be left alone by simply saying that
"We believed in this true faith" and but after this proclaim, they will
     not be tested?
Yes, Indeed.

We have certainly tested those before them, and
Allah will surely make evident those who are truthful, and
Will surely make evident the untruthful.

Do those who do evil deeds think that they can escape from Us?
What a bad judgment!
Evil is what they base on everything.

Whoever looks forward meeting with Allah,
Indeed, the scheduled time set by Allah is definitely approaching.
And Allah is the All-Hearing, the All-Knowing.

And whoever puts an effort does so only for her or his own good.
Indeed, Allah does not need anything and anyone;
Definitely, Allah is independent from all of the worlds, all of the
     creation.
[29:1–6]

Commentary

The verses focus on the concept of fear as part of the Divine way of testing people.

Discussion Question

1. How does one understand the tests, trials, and struggle in life and meeting with Allah سبحانه وتعالى after death?

Struggle

And,

The ones who struggle on Our paths
For sure, We will guide them to Our paths

Definitely and for sure,
Allah is certainly with the good, humble, forgiving and generous ones. [29:69]

Commentary

This verse is about tazkiya. Tazkiya is the process to better oneself and one's relationship with Allah سبحانه وتعالى. In the beginning of this process, the spiritual traveler can have the concepts of fear of punishment or hope of reward from Allah سبحانه وتعالى. In later stages, as the person advances through worship, good action, and knowledge in one's relationship with Allah سبحانه وتعالى, then the person now fears losing love and pleasure of Allah سبحانه وتعالى. Whatever his or her situation is, as long as Allah سبحانه وتعالى is happy and pleased with this person, this person is satisfied and have ultimate love and gratitude for Allah سبحانه وتعالى. An example of a person who fully implemented tazkiya during his entire life was the Rasulullah ﷺ. He was always in the state of gratitude and thankfulness to Allah سبحانه وتعالى in all good or evil seeming incidents. The name Muhammad literally translates as "the one who embodied gratitude and thankfulness" in Arabic language.

Discussion Questions

1. What is the importance of struggle in personal spiritual advancement in the relationship with Allah in Islam?
2. What is the most important: the struggle or the result of the struggle?

Experts of the Disciplines and Understanding the Quran

And these examples that we give for the people and
They don't truly understand their true meanings except the experts and
    specialists
[29:43]

Discussion Question

1. What is the understanding of experts in the above verse? Are they only religious experts or other experts in different fields such as natural sciences?

30.   Calmness with Your Spouse

Calmness with Your Spouse

And, it is from Allah's signs to create you from the elements on the
　　earth
Then, you spread on the earth as humans.

And, it is from Allah's signs to create for you your spouses from
　　yourself
So that you can find calmness and peace with your spouse and
Allah made between you and your spouse love and mercy
Indeed, there are signs for the people who think and ponder on all
　　these facts.
[30:20–21]

Discussion Question

    1.　What is the purpose of marriage according to the above verse?

Effect of Human's Mischief on Land and Sea

Pollution and mischief have appeared on land and sea because of what
　　humans have been doing,
For sure, Allah makes them taste the results of their action,
So that they may stop and return to the right way.
[30:41]

Commentary

Some of the scholars explain that environmental pollution occurs due
to the internal pollution of the mind and heart because of adopting
unethical behavior. One of the basic premises of Islam is respecting
everything, the nature and all human beings, due to respect to the
Divine. If this is not present, then there is internal and ethical pollution.
Therefore, external pollution becomes inevitable.

Discussion Question

    1.　How do the unethical actions of humans affect the environment
　　according to the Quran?

Cycle of Weakness and Strength in a Person's Life

Allah is the One
Who created you as a baby, being weak physically and mentally

Allah is the One
Who made you strong physically and mentally in your youth after this
weakness

Then,
Allah is the One
Who made you physically and mentally weak again in your old age
after this strength

Certainly,
Allah is the All Knower, All Powerful.
[30:54]

Discussion Question

1. How can one understand and interpret this cycle of weakness
and strength in one's life?

31. Child Education

Child Education

Oh my Child!
If there is something hidden in the size of a mustard seed, or size of an
	atom or less than that
On a rock,
In the skies,
In the space, or
On the earth,
Allah can reveal it and bring it forth.

Certainly, for sure
Allah is the Gentle, the All Knower.
[31:16]

Commentary

Above is a verse about Prophet Luqman advising his son. Prophet Luqman is instilling that Allah سبحانه وتعالى knows everything that the person does even though he or she may be alone. There is a disagreement among the Islamic scholars if Luqman was a man of wisdom and piety or a prophet assigned by Allah سبحانه وتعالى. Therefore, the person should avoid the evil and do good to please Allah سبحانه وتعالى because Allah سبحانه وتعالى is the all Knower but at the same time, Allah سبحانه وتعالى is the Gentle and always forgives the mistakes of a person as long as the person regrets and turns to Allah سبحانه وتعالى and asks forgiveness.

Discussion Question

1. How can the above verse have a critical stance in child education?

Self-Accountability

Oh humans!
Have respect, fear and love for Your Most-Wise, Protecting Rabb

Oh humans!
Prepare yourself for the Day with fear and concern,

In this Day,
Parents cannot help and save their child

In this Day,
The children cannot help and save their parents

Certainly,
The promise and pledge of Allah is true.

Therefore,
Make Sure!
Don't let this life deceive you.
and
Make Sure!
Don't let the distractions of life and evil doers take you away from
      Allah.
[31:33]

Discussion Questions

1. How does this verse emphasize the teaching of self-accountability
    in front of Allah سبحانه وتعالى؟
2. How does having a pious or evil child affect the person in front
    of Allah سبحانه وتعالى؟

32.   The Disputes and the Day of Judgment

© Lightspring/Shutterstock.com

The Disputes and the Day of Judgment

Definitely,

Your Merciful and Just Rabb

Will pass judgment on the Day of Resurrection and Accountability

About the issues that they have been arguing and disputing.
[32:25]

Discussion Questions

1.   What is the importance of believing in afterlife and account-ability after death in Islam?
2.   Is this belief similar in other religions?

33.   Abuse of the Wife

Two Things in One Heart or Two Hearts in One Person

Allah has not made for any person two hearts in one's chest cavity.
[33:4]

Commentary

According to the above verse, it is important to empty everything from the heart and put there only One Being, the Divine. In other words, the heart can and should only have Allah. If someone puts another being in the heart, that heart can become dysfunctional according to the theology. Therefore, the chants, such as "La ilaha illa Allah, there is no deity except Allah سبحانه وتعالى," constantly represent this notion of emptying and filling, because every moment a thought or a feeling enters into one's heart. If there is no effort of cleaning the heart, it will eventually die.

Discussion Question

1.   What are the methods of cleaning one's heart in Islam?

Differentiating the Role of Wife and Mother

Allah did not make your wife to be your mother
When using a word of abuse, zihar, to your wife.
[33:4]

Commentary

Although both a mother and a wife have important roles in one's life, Islam distinguishes the roles of the two for the person. This verse emphasizes the removal of the verbal abuse of the husbands to their wives by mixing the roles of a wife with one's own mother with the terminology of "zihar" practiced in early and especially pre-Islamic era. When a husband used this term for his wife by making the analogy of his wife's body parts as his mother's body parts, it was interpreted as a possible way of making divorce. In other words, his wife has become similar to his mother in their relationship.

Discussion Questions

1. Is it common for man in our time to expect the role of a wife to be similar to the role of a mother?
2. How can one understand the caretaker role of a woman as a wife compared to a mother in traditional societies?
3. What is the context of the above verse?
4. According to the context of the above verse, how can one consider the desire of a man to divorce his wife because she became old and physically unattractive? Is it considered abuse?

34. Truth and Attitude

Truth and Attitude

Say:

The truth came and after this
The falsehood cannot bring anything new
Nor it can bring anything from the past.

Say:
If I am on a wrong path
Then, definitely,
I only misguide myself to hurt myself.

If I am on guidance
Then, this will be only possible

By the virtue of what my Merciful Allah reveals to me.
Certainly,
My Gentle and Caring Rabb is all hearing and very near.
[34:49–50]

Commentary

The above verse is calling people to change their attitude; to learn, listen, and benefit their own selves.

Discussion Questions

1. What is the genuine understanding of the truth and falsehood for a person?
2. What makes a person change their own thinking, belief, attitude, and way of life?
3. According to the Quran, how can the above questions be understood?

35.   The Evil and its Outcome

If Allah makes the humans immediately accountable
For what they do,
Then, justice would demand that no human should survive on earth
But the Merciful and Forgiving Allah
Delays it to a time
When the time comes
Allah is watching over all of the creation.
[35:45]

Commentary

According to the above verses, Allah سبحانه وتعالى gives time to all humans to correct themselves for their misconducts. One of the names of Allah سبحانه وتعالى in the tradition is the Much Forbearing. This name generally comes in the scripture with another name of Allah سبحانه وتعالى, the Much Forgiver. This can mean that when Allah سبحانه وتعالى is tolerant, lenient, and patient with humans' misconduct, this can serve for them to change, regret, and repent. Then, the Forgiver forgives and erases these misconducts from the record of their deeds.

Discussion Questions

1. How does Allah سبحانه وتعالى respond to the occurrence of evil according to the above verse? Why?
2. Why is there a postponement of accountability when one does an evil action?

36.   The Embryo and The Enemy

The Embryo and The Enemy

Is the person, then, not aware that it is We who create him or her out of
a simple embryo?
After all these favors,
This person sees Us as a blatant adversary? Is this fair?

Then, the same person continues and,
Throws an example and forgets his own creation, and says:
Who can give the bones their life after they crumble on the earth after
death?

Don't Worry,
Tell them nicely:
The One who built and gave life to them before will give them life
again.
The One, Allah, is Aware, Knower, and Originator of all types of
creation.
[36:77–79]

Commentary

Above is one of the famous chapters, yasin, in the Reminder,[80] the Quran.
It is common for Muslims to read this chapter every day. This chapter is
known and practiced to bring light to the graves of the deceased loved
ones. Therefore, when a person visits a cemetery, a Muslim can read this
chapter over the buried person.

Discussion Question

1.   How does the Quran portray the logic and attitude of some
people in the above verse?

---

80. The Quran has a multitude of names and attributes referred by itself in the scripture. One
of them is the Dhikr, the Reminder.

37. Removing the Misunderstandings about Allah

Removing Misunderstandings about Allah

Pure and High is Your Rabb,
From how they wrongly describe the Divine.
The One
Who is Perfect,
Free from all false understandings and imaginations of humans.

Therefore,
Constantly, Glorify, Purify, and Correct your thoughts and feelings
    about your Pure and Glorified Rabb
With Chants and Prayers.

Therefore,
All the Peace, Blessings and Calmness are due for the sincere callers,
    messengers and prophets
For teaching the true and correct understanding of your Creator

Therefore,
Eventually and all the time,
All the Praise, Appreciation and Thanks are only truly for Allah[81]
Who is the Nourishing Rabb of all the universes, heavens and galaxies.[82]
[37:180–182]

Commentary

The above lines detach and remove all the misunderstandings about
Allah سبحانه وتعالى. In the tradition of recitation of the Quran, the
reciters end their reading generally with this line to emphasize the
correct understanding of Allah سبحانه وتعالى in theology.

Discussion Question

1. Why is it so critical and important to have the correct understanding of Allah سبحانه وتعالى in Islam?

---

81. Alhamdulillah is translated with the contextual meanings.
82. Rabbul Alamin is translated with the contextual meanings.

38.   Satan and His Mission

Critical Thinking in the Quran

The Book
That we revealed to you.
Is
A Light
A source of blessing

So that for sure,
One can ponder,
Reflect and
Think on its verses

So that, for sure
It can be a full reminder
For the smart and intelligent ones.
[38:29]

Discussion Question

1.   Why is critically thinking about the verses of the Quran emphasized so much in the Quran itself?

Satan's Judgment of His Value

Satan said:
"I am better than Adam.
You created me from fire but him from lowly dirt."
[38:76]

Discussion Question

1.   How did Satan judge the value of another creation?

Satan's Permission Request from Allah

Satan said:
"Oh my Merciful Safeguarding Rabb!
Please allow me to live till the Last Day on the earth
So that I can show You that I am right"
Allah said:
"You are granted permission
Till a known Day"
[38:79–81]

Commentary

According to the verse above, everything happens with the permission of Allah سبحانه وتعالى and there is a wisdom and reason behind it.

Discussion Question

1. Why was Satan so determined in his mission of showing his superiority over Adam (PBUH)?

39.   Opening the Chest and Heart

The Chest

When Allah opens the person's chest, soul and heart for the true
    guidance, and submission, then, this person is now on the
    peaceful, delightful path of joy and happiness, from her or his
    Loving and Nourishing Rabb

After this,
How unfortunate are the ones whose hearts become hardened due to
    not remembering Allah?

These ones are on a clear misguidance.
[39:22]

Commentary

The above verse is presented with its transliteration. The red transliterated text from Arabic is presented to allude to the original sounds with the
experiential meanings in practice. Some of the people in practice, especially some Sufis, read this verse in the mornings when he or she wakes
up in order to open one's spiritual heart. In other words, some have ex-
perienced that if a person reads it early in the morning before eating and
talking, this verse has its own way of emulating spiritual heart surgery
for spiritual expansion.

Discussion Questions

1. How do the sounds have effect on the human heart and mind?
2. How does the word "sharaha" echo without knowing the meaning
    of it? How does this sound correspond with its meaning?"
3. Why is it suggested to read certain phrases in the original
    language of revelation?

True Appreciation of the Divine

They were not showing true Appreciation for Allah
The whole earth will be of a single grip with the Exalted Most High
    Merciful Allah on the Day of Judgment, and
The heavens will be rolled up like a paper with the order of the Creator.
Pure is Allah,
Far too high than what they falsely associate with
The Unique One Allah.
[39:67]

Commentary

The above verse can indicate awe and appreciation for Allah سبحانه
وتعالى. In the Quran, there are verses that praise Christians and Jews and
any person on the journey, crying at night and using different tools such
as scriptures, prayers, chants, and reflection to establish and maintain a
relationship with the Creator in order to appreciate and be thankful to
Allah سبحانه وتعالى.

Discussion Question

1. How can one show appreciation and thankfulness to Allah
    سبحانه وتعالى in Islam?

40.   Proving their superiority by argument?

For sure, and clearly,
The ones who argue about Our verses and signs
Without any proof, logic, and reference

They do it only to show their superiority, and how great they are!
Don't worry,
They won't be able to reach the level of superiority that they desire.

After all this,
Seek refuge in Allah from their evil and harm.

Certainly,
Allah is Fully Aware, Hearing and Seeing.
[40:56]

Discussion Questions

1. How can one understand the arguments about religion in the light of the above verse?
2. According to the above verse, what is authentic? What is the true knowledge and information about Allah سبحانه وتعالى؟

41.   The Straight Path and Consistency

The Straight Path and Consistency

For sure, the ones who say
"Our Merciful and All Caring Rabb is Allah"
Then,
They continue on the straight path and middle way, and,
The angels descend on them and say:
"Don't worry, and don't be scared"
"Be happy with the heaven that is promised for you"
"We are your friends in this world and afterlife"
"You will get what you desire…."
"You will get what you want…."
"This is from the One who is the Most Forgiving, and the Most
    Merciful."
After all this,
Who has the best word and approach
Other than the ones:
Praying and appreciating Allah,
Always doing good
And saying
"I am from the Muslims, the ones who fully turned themselves over
    to Allah and accepted everything from the One and Only True
    Merciful Creator."
[41:30–33]

Discussion Questions

1. How can angels become friends of a person on the path?
2. Why do angels console a person on the path?

Humility

Among Allah's signs are the night and the day, and the sun and the
   moon.
Do not prostrate yourselves to the sun, or to the moon, or anything
   else.
But prostrate yourselves to Allah who has created them,
If you only, and sincerely worship your One Rabb.
Still, if they continue to show arrogance,
Then, those who are in the Loving, Merciful and Exalted Divine
   Presence
Worship Allah, day and night, and
They do not get tired but take pleasure, sweetness and taste from it.
[41:37–38]

Discussion Question

1. How can one show humbleness and humility for Allah سبحانه
   وتعالى in prayers?

Language of the Scripture

And if we made this Quran in another language other than Arabic
Then, they for sure would have said
"Shouldn't its verses be understood and explained?"
So, it will be a non-Arabic Book to an Arab messenger?
Does this make sense?

After this,
Tell them:
This Quran is a guidance and
A source of health for the ones who attained faith.
But as for those who won't believe,
In their ears is deafness, and
This book will be invisible and obscure to them.
As if they are being called from a very far distance.
[41:44]

Discussion Question

1. How does the above verse rationalize the language of the
    Quran?

42.   How Allah Communicates with Humans

How Allah Communicates with Humans

And,
It is not possible for any mortal human that Allah speaks to this person
Except
By revelation

Or

From behind a veil with a means of a vehicle

Or

By sending a messenger (i.e., angel) with a revelation

Communicating the Divine messages with the permission of Allah.

After all, certainly,
Allah is Exalted, far from human thoughts and imaginations,
Allah is the source of Wisdom and Authority.
[42:51]

Discussion Questions

1.   In Islam, according to the above verse, how can one understand
     Allah سبحانه وتعالى's communication with humans? Why?
2.   Will the way of communication of Allah سبحانه وتعالى with the
     person change after death? How?

43.   Angels and Speculations

Angels and Speculations

And,
They made false claims about angels:
By asserting that they are females.
They are only the creation and worshippers of Allah, the Most
    Merciful.
When they claim this,
Did they witness the creation of angels?

What a false claim!

They will soon be questioned
About their assertions.
[43:19]

Commentary

In Islam, it is important to believe in the unseen without any speculations. A person can know about the unseen from the information which Allah سبحانه وتعالى provides in the scriptures. The first and foremost unseen is Allah سبحانه وتعالى. A Muslim should follow the guidelines in the scripture about who Allah سبحانه وتعالى is. Repeatedly verses of the Quran contain the following statement, which is an order from Allah سبحانه وتعالى to Rasulullah ﷺ to convey the message of Who Allah سبحانه وتعالى is: "Tell them that it has been revealed that your Creator is One." Or in the chapter of unity [112], "Tell them that Allah سبحانه وتعالى is One and Unique. Allah سبحانه وتعالى was not born and does not give birth." Similarly, the life after death, angels, future, and destiny are some examples of the unseen as well. The above verse explains that people make speculations about angels by putting a gender on them and there is no information revealed about this claim of some humans. The verse refutes their claim.

Discussion Question

1. How can one increase his or her knowledge about the unseen
    with a genuine or authentic methodology in Islam?

44.   Signs before the Termination of the Earth

Signs before the Termination of the Earth

After this,
Wait and expect the day
When the sky is covered with an obvious smoke.
[44:10]

Commentary

According to an expected prophecy by the Prophet[11], one of the signs before the full annihilation of the earth[83] is the sky being covered with smoke. The verse above mentions this prophecy. The name of this chapter is called "The Smoke" due to this verse.

Discussion Question

1. What are the other signs before full termination of earth according to the Quran and Hadith?

---

83. Which is referred to as "end of time."

45.   Accountability

Accountability

And that day
You will see
All groups, peoples, communities
Humbling themselves before Allah by kneeling down,
All groups, people, and communities
Are being called to their records of accountability.

Today,
You will be rewarded or held accountable for
What you have been doing on the earth in your life.
[45:28]

Commentary

The above verse explains group as well as individual accountability. It is very important in Islam to side with the groups of ethical behavior and action, although people may have different beliefs. However, as mentioned in Chapter 3, the Quran additionally calls Christians, Jews, and Muslims to the recognition and acceptance of their common One Creator and accordingly work together for the good, not falsehood.

Discussion Question

1. What is the difference between group and individual accountability in front of Allah سبحانه وتعالى in Islam?

46.   The Mother, the Father, and the Child

The Mother, the Father, and the Child

We required the person
To be nice, grateful and kind to his/her parents

This person's mother had a pregnancy and delivery,
With difficulty and pain,

And, even with difficulty
Pregnancy and breastfeeding
Can take up to thirty months.
[46:15]

Commentary

According to some of the commentators of the Quran, three months
is the time when the soul of the person is blown into the baby after
the conception. Therefore, recognition of the personhood of the baby
can come after the first three months. The remaining period adds up to
thirty months: six months remaining of the nine months of pregnancy
and twenty-four months of the breastfeeding period.

Discussion Questions

1. What is the right of a mother and father in relation to the child
   in Islam?
2. How can one understand the Quran's specific numbers
   regarding pregnancy, child formation in the womb, and
   breastfeeding? How can one compare it with current scientific
   data in gynecology?

47.   Know That There Is No Deity except Allah

Know That There Is No Deity except Allah

After all this,

Know certainly without any doubt!
That
There is no deity, god, except Allah.

And, therefore,

Constantly be in the state of asking forgiveness
For your forgetfulness, heedlessness and carelessness in your
      relationship
With your true, only, very Merciful and Caring and One Allah

And, also ask forgiveness
For your fellow brothers and sisters as well.

Allah knows your change
From one place to another
From one spiritual state to another
From one struggle to another

And,

Allah also knows your place of station
Where you will end in this world.
Where you will end in the afterlife.
[47:19]

Discussion Questions

1. Why is the full belief in One Allah سبحانه وتعالى the core of
    Islam? How does the above verse represent this creed?
2. How can one understand the change and station in the above
    verse?

48.   Tranquility and Calmness on the Heart

Tranquility and Calmness on the Heart

Allah is the One who
Poured tranquility[84] and calmness into the hearts of the believers

So that,

Their existing belief and trust in Allah can increase
With more and more trust and belief.

And Remember!
All the forces of the skies and earth belong to Allah

And Remember!
Allah is always All Knowing, All Source of Wisdom and Authority.
[48:4]

Discussion Question

1.   What is the correct understanding of tranquility or sakina in
     the heart of a person in Islam? How can the tranquility reach
     and establish itself in this heart of a person?

---

84. Sakina in Ar.

49.   Social and Ethnic Classifications

Social and Ethnic Classifications

Oh people!
Indeed,
We have created you as males and females.

And after that,
We put you in different nations, social, ethnic and kinship groups

So that,
You have the interest and motivation to know each other.

But Remember!
Certainly and for sure,
The best and highest of you among all of these groups
Is the one who has appreciation, and consciousness of Allah

Indeed, Remember!
Allah is All Knowing, All Aware of your Engagements.
[49:13]

Commentary

The true consciousness of Allah سبحانه وتعالى is only known by Allah
سبحانه وتعالى. Therefore, no one has the authority in a real sense to judge
or value any other person except Allah سبحانه وتعالى. This approach
eliminates any type of discrimination in social life according to Islam.

Discussion Question

1. What is the purpose of different ethnic, national, and social
    classifications according to Islam?

50.   **Escape from Death**

Closer than Jugular Veins

Certainly,
We created the person and
We know what type of temptations one's own self constantly whispers
    and
We are closer to this person than this person's own jugular veins
[50:16]

Discussion Question

1.   What does being closer to someone than "this person's own
jugular veins" mean?

The Intoxication of Death

The intoxication of death[85] has now come for sure,
That was the part you always tried to escape.
[50:19]

Discussion Question

1.   What does the intoxication of death mean in theology?

---

85. Sakratul Mawt in Ar.

51.   Escape to Allah

Escape to Allah

After all this,
"Escape to Allah!
Run to Allah!"

Certainly and for sure,
I am an obvious and straightforward
Warning Messenger
To you from Allah
[51:50]

Commentary

In the previous chapter, 50, the same word for escape is used—"firar" in Arabic. When one connects two consecutive chapters for the same contextual meaning, escaping from death to Allah سبحانه وتعالى may appear. Especially in Sufi terminology, this word, firar, escape from, has embedded meanings.

Discussion Question

1.   What does "escaping or running" to Allah سبحانه وتعالى mean in the above verse?

Benefit of Advice

After all this, give them advice!
For sure,
Advice will benefit at least some, who have attained faith in Allah.
And remember!
"I created the Jinn[86] and humans only to
Recognize, appreciate, and worship Me."
[51:55–56]

Discussion Question

1.   What is the etiquette of giving advice in Islam?

---

86.   Jinn are other creations of Allah other than humans. They are also accountable for their actions and choices in life. They are unseen creatures from a unique creation often thought of as ghost like creatures.

52.   Allah as the Just and the Merciful in Accountability

And that Day, after the completion of questioning and accountability,

They will be dragged to imprisonment and punishment.

The officers will say:

"Isn't this the punishment that you were denying its existence in your
life on the earth?

Look now! Is this punishment magic or illusion? Don't you see now?

You will be imprisoned and punished and it doesn't matter if you are
patient or not.

As a justice, you are all being paid back now for your ungratefulness
to Allah, your evil and oppression to other humans and all other
creations that you have been constantly preoccupied with in the
world."

On the contrary,

Certainly and for sure,
The ones who are respectful of Allah and being ethical, just and fair to
humans
Will be in gardens and pleasure
Enjoying what their Generous and Merciful Rabb has given them, and
Their Caring and Appreciative Rabb protected them from the
punishment and imprisonment.

The friendly officers will say:
"Indulge in all pleasures, eating, drinking....
With the mercy of Allah,
You are all being paid back now
For your regular respect and worship of Allah,
For being ethical, just and fair to humans and all other creations,
Which you were persistently being preoccupied with in the world."
[52:13–19]

Discussion Question

1. How can one understand the names of Allah سبحانه وتعالى in Islam as the Just and the Merciful, according to the above verse, and others?

53.   Following a Fantasy

The Star

With the name of Allah, the All-Merciful, the Very-Merciful.
By the star, when it goes down to set,
[53:1]

Commentary

In the scripture, there are a lot of referrals to night journeys. In the Book of Allah سبحانه وتعالى, the Quran, there are chapter names with The Night, The Star, The Moon, and The Sun. As the Quran mentions, the physical and spiritual journeys of Moses سبحانه وتعالى and Muhammad صلى الله عليه وسلم happened at night. The burning bush was at night.

Discussion Question

1.   What is the significance of stars according to the Quran?

Following a Fantasy

For sure,
These are the names
That you and your forefathers made up about Allah.
Allah did not send any proof about it.
They just follow an ungrounded fantasy.
They just follow what their egos' desire
About knowing Allah.

However, think and look!
Certainly,
The Guidance, the Quran, came to them from their Merciful Rabb.
[53:23]

Discussion Question

1.   Is it common for people to call Allah سبحانه وتعالى according to their own deductions? According to the above verse and others, what makes those deductions about Allah سبحانه وتعالى true or whimsical?

54.   The Easy Quran

The Easy Quran

And,
For Sure and Definitely,
We made the Quran easy in mind
As a Book of Remembrance
As a Book of Chant
As a Book of Worship
As a Book of Advice

After all this,
Is there anyone who will take it to the heart?
Is there anyone who will take advice from it?
Is there anyone of who will take it as a book of chant and worship?
[54:17, 22, 32, 40]

Commentary

The above verse is repeated four times in this chapter.

Discussion Questions

1.   What is the purpose of repetition in the Quran according to the exegetical scholars?
2.   What are the different names of the Quran? Why?

55. Which favors of your Merciful, Nourishing, and Caring Rabb will you deny?

Which favors of your Merciful, Nourishing, and Caring Rabb will you deny?

After all this,

Which favors of your Merciful, Nourishing, and Caring Rabb will you
deny?

[55:13, 16, 18, 21, 23, 25, 28, 30, 32, 34, 36, 38, 40, 42, 45, 47, 49, 51, 53,
55, 57, 59, 61, 63, 65, 67, 69, 71, 73, 75, 77]

Commentary

The above verse is repeated thirty-one times in the above chapter. The
address is for men, women, and the Jinn.[87] After each bounty cited in the
chapter, the above verse occurs. This chapter is in a different style than
the other chapters of the Quran.

Discussion Questions

1. What is the importance of this chapter in practice?
2. How can one compare the style of this chapter with other
    chapters in the Quran?

The Sun and Moon by Precise Calculation

Ar-Rahman,

The Most Merciful and the Most Caring,

Taught you the Quran.

Created the person.

Taught this person how to speak and express him or herself.

Remember!

The sun and the moon are on a specific orbit with precise calculation.

[55:1–5]

---

87. The Jinn are the unseen creation of Allah similar to humans. The Jinn also have their own
life span, the free will, and accountability of their actions in front of Allah.

Discussion Questions

1. As the chapter starts with one of the names of Allah سبحانه وتعالى, the Most Merciful and the Most Caring, Ar-Rahman, what can be the reason for this type of beginning for this chapter?

2. How can one interpret the understanding of the precise calculation of the sun and moon in the above verse?

56.   Coordinates of Stars in the Universe

© ARCHITECTEUR/Shutterstock.com

Drinking Pure Wine

They will drink bowls and jugs and a goblet of pure wine,
From which they will neither suffer headache,
Nor will they be intoxicated.
[56:18–19]

Commentary

In the above description, one of the drinks in Heaven will be wine. It will only give pleasure. There will not be any side effects from it. There will not be any pain of headache, migraine, or vomitin,g unlike other alcoholic drinks in this world. The worldly pleasures can have side effects, but the pleasures in Heaven will be without it. According to the Muslim mystics, Sufis, a person drinks a better spiritual wine in life compared to the normal wine if one gets intoxicated with the spiritual ecstasy of the Divine.

Discussion Questions

1. What is the difference between physical and spiritual intoxication?
2. How can one taste a better pleasure by being spiritually intoxicated in the practice compared to drinking wine?

Coordinates of Stars in the Universe

After this,

I swear and affirm on the precise location, coordinates of each star in the universe.

And Certainly and Absolutely,

This affirmation is an enormous and critical statement if you scientifically know.

Certainly and definitely,

This is the Noble Quran,

This Quran is well-protected and guarded, original and pure.

Therefore,

The impure should not touch it.

[56:75–79]

Commentary

In the above verses, Allah سبحانه وتعالى is underlining the importance of coordinates of each star in the galaxies in the balance of all the systems of the universe. Muslims cannot touch the original revelation of the Quran in Arabic unless they physically perform a washing ritual called wudhu or ghusl. The verse "the impure should not touch it" indicates this ruling in Islam.

Discussion Question

1. What is the importance and interpretation of coordinates of each star in present astronomy? How can one interpret this information with the above verse?

57.   Hardened Hearts and Remembrance of Allah

© shiva3d/Shutterstock.com

Hardened Hearts and Remembrance of Allah

Has the time not come for the believers and appreciators of Allah
That their hearts be humble and tremble at the remembrance of Allah
And even all the truth is revealed to them?

After this,
Do not be like those who are given the Divine revelations before
And still their hearts become hardened after a long time passed
And most of them are lost-wanderers.[88]
[57:16]

Commentary

The above line is mentioned in the chapter of iron. One of the isotopes
of iron in the periodic table is 57. The chapter of iron has the number
of 57. According to the modern commentators, this is one of the many
miracles of the Quran. Also, it is interesting to note that the verse is
mentioned in the chapter of iron and Allah سبحانه وتعالى is mentioning
hearts becoming hardened due to not remembering Allah سبحانه وتعالى.
In practice, if a person does not have regular rituals, prayer, chanting, or
practice in remembrance of Allah سبحانه وتعالى, the heart of the person

---

88. Fasiq is translated as lost wanderer due to the context of the verse.

will be hardened and will be susceptible and vulnerable to different spiritual diseases.

Discussion Questions

1. How does one's heart become hardened physically and spiritually?
2. How does remembrance of Allah سبحانه وتعالى soften one's heart in practice?

58.   Secret Conversations

Secret Conversations

Have you not observed that Allah knows everything in the skies, in
    space, in the galaxies and everything in the earth?
No secret conversation takes place between three, but Allah is the
    fourth of them,
Nor between five, but Allah is the sixth of them,
Neither between fewer than that nor more,
But Allah is with them wherever they are.
Then at the end,
Allah will tell them on the Day of Judgment what they did.
Surely, Allah is All-Knowing and All Aware about everything.
[58:7]

Discussion Question

    1.   What is the ethical teaching of the above verse in Islam?

59.   Self and Allah

Self and Allah

Oh you who believe in Allah!
Have respect, and appreciation for Allah!

Every person should consider
What they prepare for tomorrow
What they prepare for tomorrow
For the Day of Judgement

Have respect and appreciation of Allah!
   Allah is aware of what you are constantly engaged in.

Don't be like the ones that forget Allah
Then, Allah made them forget their own selves

These are the lost wanderers.[89]
[59:18–19]

Discussion Question

1.   If a person forgets oneself does the person forget Allah سبحانه
وتعالى as well?

---

89. Fasiq is translated as lost wanderer due to the context of the verse.

60.   Enemies Becoming Friends

Enemies Becoming Friends

It is possible that
Allah can make friendship
Between you and your enemies
Allah is All Powerful to do anything.

After this, Remember!
Indeed,
Allah is All Forgiving about the past if you sincerely regret, repent and
     ask forgiveness
Because
Allah is All Merciful and Caring about the creation.
[60:7]

Discussion Questions

1.   What is the message of the above verse?
2.   How do the Muslims incorporate the teaching of this verse in
       their lives?
3.   What is the story of the serial killer who killed one hundred
       people in the hadith tradition?

61.   Advising What You Don't Practice

Advising What You Don't Practice

Oh you who attained faith in Allah
Why do you say things and advise people
That you don't do and practice yourself.

Most loathsome in the sight of Allah are the ones
Who advise people
But they don't do themselves
[61:2–3]

Discussion Question

1.   What should be the ethics of counseling others according to the
     above verse?

62.   Run Away from Death

Say,
For sure,
the death that you are trying to run away from
Definitely will visit you as well.
After,
You will be returned to
the One, Knower of all Unseen and Unknowns,
the One, Knower of all Seen and Knowns.
So that,
The One, Allah will inform about the true reality of your engagements
in the world.
[62:8]

Discussion Question

1.   Why does the person want to escape from death?

63.   Not Worshipping Allah Due to Being Busy

Not Worshipping Allah Due to Being Busy

Oh You who attained faith and trust in Allah!
Make sure your preoccupation
With your work
With your family
Do not stop you from remembering, and worshipping your
All Merciful and All Caring Creator
Whoever stops appreciating and remembering Allah
For sure,
This person becomes only a loser in this world and afterlife.
[63:9]

Discussion Questions

1. Is it common for people to stop their religious duties due to their preoccupations with work and family?
2. What is the teaching of the verse above accordingly?

64. As Much as You Can

As Much as You Can

After all this,
Have fear, love and respect of Allah
As much as you can!

Pay attention!
Follow the teachings of Allah,
Help the poor and needy
All above are good and beneficial for you.

After all this,
Whoever protects oneself
From his or her own caprice, misery, and evil

Then,
It is those who will be
Happy and successful.
In this life and after death.
[64:16]

Discussion Questions

1. What does "having fear, respect and love of Allah سبحانه وتعالى as much as you can" mean in practice and theology of Islam according to the above verse?
2. What is the caprice and evil of one toward one's own self in the above verse?

65.   Financial Concerns in Divorce

© zimmytws/Shutterstock.com

Financial Concerns in Divorce

And remember!
For all the financial concerns in divorce,
Allah can provide livelihood, sustenance and money
From a source that this person does not expect at all,

After all this,
Whoever truly relies and trusts in Allah
Allah is sufficient for that person.
For sure,
Allah's decision is always and perfectly fulfilled.

And remember!
For sure and definitely,
Allah makes balance in everything.
[65:3]

Commentary

The above lines are from the verse that contextually mentions the difficulties of divorce and its financial concerns and conflicts between the spouses before, during, and after the process. It is important to remember that Allah سبحانه وتعالى can provide livelihood and sustenance for the person who may be much concerned about the financial burden of divorce during its process and after it.

Discussion Question

1. Is it common for people to keep or break their marriages due to financial fears?

66.   Two Model Women: Virgin Mary and the Wife of Pharaoh

The Wife of Pharaoh

And Remember,
Allah brings a model for the believers
The example of the wife of the pharaoh

When she said secretly:
"Oh my Protecting and Just Rabb, prepare a royal residence for me in
     Heaven and
Save me from pharaoh and his oppression and
Save me from the group of oppressors."
[66:11]

Commentary

One of the role model women is the wife of pharaoh in Islam. She was not supporting her husband for his oppression toward the children of Israel. She was secretly making prayer to Allah سبحانه وتعالى to ask forgiveness and an opportunity to be protected from the evil and oppression of pharaoh in this world and in the afterlife. It is important in theology not to support the oppressors. According to the Prophet, there are three levels of changing and not supporting the evil. The first level is stopping evil by all means of effort. The lower level is stopping it verbally, by talking against it. The lowest level is by detesting the evil action even though you're not doing anything about it [11].

Discussion Question

1.   Why is the position of wife of pharaoh special in Islam?

Virgin Mary

And Remember,
Allah brings a model for the believers
The example of Virgin Mary, the daughter of Joachim.

Virgin Mary is the one
Who protected her chastity and piety
And accordingly,
From Our pool of the souls,
We breathed a soul into Jesus.
Then,
Virgin Mary
Testified and witnessed to the truth of the words of her
Merciful Rabb and the Divine books,
She was one of the pious and devout in appreciating the favors of
    Allah.
[66:12]

Discussion Question

1. How is the birth of Jesus according to the verse above and others
    in Islamic theology?

67. Birds

© Yurchenko Yulia/Shutterstock.com

Birds

Don't they see the birds above them,
Flying in groups, spreading and folding their wings,
With involuntary and voluntary drives,
None but the Most Merciful and Gracious One holds them in the air
Definitely, Allah is aware and watchful of everything
[67:19]

Discussion Question

1. How do Muslims interpret scientific explanations about natural events?

68.   Grasping with the Eyes

The ones who are bent on denying the truth would almost grasp and
    kill you with their eyes whenever they hear this reminder...
[68:51]

Commentary

The above line is an example of the effect of the evil eye on humans.
Islam accepts the effects of the evil eye and suggests some ways to be
protected from it. Some Muslims can print above expressions from the
Quran and place them in different parts of the house, office, or vehicle.
Some Sufis carry different phrases in their bags or pockets so as to be
protected from evil and attract the good. Alternatively, they read daily
some litanies or prayers of protection with the suggestion of the Prophet.

Discussion Question

1.   What does "grasping with their eyes" in the above verse mean?

69. Very Little Thinking, Reflection, and Belief

Very Little

For sure and definitely,

This book is the word of a
Noble Messenger and
Not the word of a poet but
Very little you believe

And this book is
Not the word of a magician but
Very little you think and reflect

Revealed in pieces from the
the Merciful and Caring Rabb of all the universe, heavens and galaxies.
[69:40–43]

Discussion Question

1. What does the word "very little" signify in critical thinking in
   the above verse according to the exegetical interpretations?

And for Sure

And for sure,
this Book is a Reminder
For the ones
who have respect, humbleness, and fairness

And for sure,
Definitely, We know that
Some of you will not accept and will deny

And for sure,
This Book is disappointing for the deniers

And for sure,
This Book is certainly the absolute Truth

After all this,
Don't worry about them!
Move on!
Turn to your Merciful Rabb
Glorify and Connect to
Your Rabb
With the Most Exalted and Highest Name
[69:48–52]

Discussion Questions

1. In the above verse, how can one interpret the notion of "certainty"? Why?
2. How can a person use the scripture for others and for oneself?

70.   Elevators and Paths

Elevators and Paths

From Allah,
There are countless elevators and paths
In order to spiritually climb up.
[70:3]

Commentary

The above rendering is similar to the rendering of Muhammad Asad[13]. The verse encourages everyone to find a way to establish a relationship with Allah سبحانه وتعالى. There are a lot of paths to spiritually excel in establishing a relationship with the Divine.

Discussion Question

1.   What is meant by "elevators and paths" in the above verse?

71.   My House

My House

Oh my Merciful, Safeguarding, and Caring Rabb
Forgive me,
Forgive my parents
Forgive everyone who enters my house as a person of appreciation and
    believer of You
Forgive all the men and women who appreciates and attains faith in
    You

And as for the oppressors, the evil doers and evil planners
Counter their evil and oppression with a satisfactory and better
    encounter
[71:28]

Commentary

Above is a prayer of Prophet Noah عليه السلام mentioned in the Quran.
He asks forgiveness from Allah سبحانه وتعالى for everyone. As the Prophet
Noah عليه السلام and his followers were weak in the society they were
not able to counter the oppression against the oppressors except asking
and praying to Allah سبحانه وتعالى for protection against their evil. In
Arabic, there are different words for house such as al-bayt which is used
in this verse. Another word for house is maskan which means the place
of tranquility, calmness, and sakina.

Discussion Questions

1.   What is the place of a house in Islam?
2.   How can one interpret the above prayer of asking blessing from
     Allah سبحانه وتعالى for the visitors and guests coming to one's
     house?

72.   The unseen beings and the humans, dare to lie against Allah?

The unseen beings and the humans, dare to lie against Allah?

The unseen beings, Jinns said:
"And,
Certainly,
Our Merciful Rabb is Exalted, the Most High
Does not have any children
Does not have any equivalent or spouse.
And,
But still the ignorant ones among us
Are saying nonsense things about Allah.

And,
Indeed,
We thought that
The humans and the Jinn, unseen beings[90]
Will not dare to lie against Allah."
[72:3–5]

Discussion Questions

1. What are the unseen beings?
2. Who is we in the above verse?
3. What do the unseen beings find nonsense for the claims about
    Allah سبحانه وتعالى؟

---

90. Jinn is translated as unseen beings similar to rendering of M. Asad [13]. Like humans, Jinn have their own life, death, and accountability in front of Allah.

73.   Importance of Nights Compared to Daytime

Importance of Nights Compared to Daytime

The time spent at *Night*
in worship,
in chant and
in prayers to Allah
is
More strong and satisfactory
For heart and tongue
Compared to the *Daytime*
Because, for sure,
You get busy in the day time.
[73:6–7]

Commentary

There is a lot of encouragement for night prayers and worship in the Quran and in the sayings of the Rasulullah .

Discussion Question

1. Why are the night prayers more valuable compared to daytime prayers in Islam?

74. Clean Dress, Clean Body, and Clean Heart

Clean Dress, Clean Body, and Clean Heart

Oh who is secluded, folded and cloaked
Get up and inform people about Allah
Glorify the Greatness of your Merciful and Nourishing Creator
Always keep your dress and heart clean
Always keep your body and heart away from filth and evil

After this,
Do not compromise from your principles to acquire more
But
Continue to be patient
In the path of your Merciful and Caring Allah.
[74:1–7]

Discussion Question

1. How is external cleanliness related to internal cleanliness in Islam? How is this principle applied in five daily prayers for Muslims?

75. Fingerprints

© PRESSLAB/Shutterstock.com

Fingerprints

I swear by the Day of Resurrection
And I swear by the self-blaming self
Does man think that We cannot assemble his or her bones?
Yes, certainly We can do it.
Even, We can resurrect the humans from their fingerprints.
[75:1–4]

Commentary

By using the above verse, modern interpreters explain that the Quran explains miraculously 1,400 years ago about the uniqueness of each person's fingerprints. Due to this reason, in our present time, since each person has different fingerprints, a person can be identified with this in the field of criminology.

Discussion Question

1. How do the modern commentators explain and interpret the Quran with new scientific and technologies discoveries?

Self-Awareness

For sure,
The person is aware of their own self
But at the same time makes up excuses
[75:14–15]

Discussion Question

1. Is the self-awareness mentioned in the above verse in this life or after death?

76.   The Human Being

The Human Being

Don't you know
Billions of years passed
Human being was not
Worthy of mention

Then, We created the human
From a microscopic size embryo
Then, testing this person
While this person seeing and hearing

We gave this person a free choice
A choice of recognition and appreciation
Or a choice of unrecognition and unappreciation
[76:1–3]

Discussion Questions

1. What is the original word for "billions of years" in the scripture? Does this word have any significance in the literature?
2. To what does recognition and appreciation in the translation refer?

77.   Embarrassment, Humiliation, and Denying the Truth

Embarrassment, Humiliation, and Denying the Truth

Didn't We create you from a simple water, a fluid of sperm?
Then, We put this with the egg in a firm place, to the womb.
Till to a known time of pregnancy and delivery

After all,
We determined everything!
How excellent everything We arranged and determined!

After all this,
If they don't recognize and appreciate Allah
How embarrassing and humiliated are those
On that Day
Who deny these truths
[77:20–24]

Commentary

The expression "how embarrassing are those on that Day who deny these truths" is repeated ten times in this chapter.

Discussion Question

1. What could be reasons of repetition for the above expression in this chapter?

Which word after this Quran?

When they are told to
Show Appreciation and Respect to Allah
By worship and bowing

If they still don't do it
How embarrassing and humiliated are those
On that Day
Who deny these truths

After all this,
If they don't believe in this Quran
Which other word will they believe in?
[77:48–50]

Discussion Question

1. What is the position of the Quran compared to other words in Islamic theology?

78.   The Great Event

The Great Event

Do you know about what they are asking each other all the time?
About the Great Event!
About which they speculate and dispute
Don't Worry!
Certainly, they will know soon about it
Don't Worry!
For sure,
They will know soon about it.
[78:1–5]

For Sure,
This Day, the Great Event
Is True and Real.
After all this,
Whoever wants
Can prepare an acceptable path
To their Merciful, Forgiving and Caring Rabb
[78:39]

Commentary

Great Event is another name of the Day of resurrection and accountability after death.

Discussion Question

1.   What is the teaching of the Prophet about the Last Day of the earth and the Day of resurrection?

79.   **Extractors**

(Soul) Extractors

With the name of Allah, the All-Merciful, the Very-Merciful.
I swear by those who extract with great force
I swear by those who extract smoothly
I swear by those who float and swim swiftly,
Then, those who compete with each other
Then, those who arrange the matters
On the Day, when the shocking event will shock everything
[79:1–6]

Discussion Question

1.   What is the context of actions in the above verses?

80.   Preference in Teaching

He frowned and turned away
When the blind came
How do you know
Maybe the blind will benefit from the spiritual purification
When reminded about Allah
Maybe even this reminder will have a benefit

But,
The one who is arrogant and does not care
You give attention to this person

While no blame is expected of you
If this arrogant person does not attain any purity.
[80:1–7]

Discussion Question

1.   According to the above verse, who should be given preference
to teach when someone wants to learn?

81.   Wrapping up the Sun

Wrapping up the Sun

With the name of Allah, the All-Merciful, the Very-Merciful.
When the sun is wrapped up and
When the stars are fallen down and
When the mountains are set in motion,
When all the valuables[91] are abandoned and
When all the wild animals are gathered and
When the seas are lit up with fire and
When all the humans are paired with their engagements and
When the murdered female children will be resurrected and
        questioned
about their murderer and for what sin she was killed for and
When the scrolls (of deeds) will be unscrolled and
When the sky will be ripped off and
When the punishments are prepared and
When Heaven and rewards are brought close

NOW
The soul knows what it has brought
and which direction it is going
[81:1–14]

Discussion Question

1. How can one interpret the content and style of the above verses
    compared to other texts?

---

91. I'saru in all the translations are as pregnant camel. It has the contextual meaning of being
a very valuable asset for the Arabs. Therefore, contextual meaning was preferred for the
contemporary time.

82. Deception

Deception

Oh man!
What is constantly deceiving you about your Gracious, Loving, and
Merciful Rabb
Who created you,
Then perfected you,
Then made you in balance and proportion
In a form, color, face, and body according to the Divine choice

After all this,
Are you still denying the religion, the Day of Judgment and
Accountability?
No!
(For sure, you are making a huge mistake!
And,
Still tempting to tell a lie and use an excuse)
[82:6–9]

Discussion Questions

1. How do the above verses establish connection between the creation of the human beings and the need of a religion and accountability after death?
2. What is the significance of this chapter?
3. What are the different themes covered in this chapter?

83.   Cheating

Shame on those!
Who cheat and deceive people
But when they receive their due from people
They demand in full
But, when their due is to give,
They give less than it's due

Do they not know that they will be raised from the dead? and
Called for accountability on an Overpowering Nerve Wrecking Day!
The Day,
When all men shall stand before the Creator and Sustaining Rabb of all
        the worlds and universes!
[83:1–6]

Discussion Question

1.   How can understanding and interpretation of above verses help
     the person live an ethical life?

84. Earth, Sky, and Their Relationship with Allah

Earth and Sky and Their Relationship with Allah

With the name of Allah, the All-Merciful, the Very-Merciful

When the sky cracks and splits and
Listens to the command of its All-Powerful Rabb
As it should listen and

When the earth is stretched
And throws up and empties whatever it contains, and
Listens to the command of its All-Powerful Rabb
As it should listen

(See now! what every person has brought forth for their struggle in
    life)

Oh man!
You are in constant engagement and struggle
Until you meet with your Merciful and Just Rabb
Finally, and Certainly,
You will meet with your Creator
[84:1–6]

Discussion Question

    1. How does the above verse portray the position of the sky and
       the earth in their relationship with Allah سبحانه وتعالى؟

85. Love of Allah

Love of Allah

For sure, the grasp of your Merciful Safeguarding Rabb is so strong
For sure, Allah is the One who creates, re-creates and resurrects
And for sure, Allah is the Most-Forgiving, the Most-Loving,
And for sure, Allah is the Owner of the Exalted Authority, Control and
    Dominion
[85:12–15]

Discussion Question

1. How is the love of Allah سبحانه وتعالى understood in Islam
    compared to Christianity, Judaism, and other religions?

86.   Human Fertilization and Implantation

© Puwadol Jaturawutthichai/Shutterstock.com

Human Fertilization and Implantation

Does the person look what he or she was created from?
Created from a discharged fluid of sperm and an egg
Coming from between the loins and the pelvic arch
Of a man and a woman
For a human fertilization and implantation

After all this,
Certainly, definitely, and for sure,
Allah has the power to recreate after death
For a Day,
Where all the secrets are exposed
And the person does not have
Neither strength nor supporter or helper

Here is another example:

For sure, when the sky sends the rain like sperm
For sure, when the earth cracks open like an egg
For a fertilization and implantation

After all this,
Certainly, for sure and definitely,
This Quran is a separator between the truth and falsehood

I swear
This is not a joke!
[86:5–14]

Discussion Questions

1. Why is there so much emphasis on recreation and accountability after death in the Quran?
2. How do the current Quranic commentators explain the above verses with the advent of the science of reproduction and embryology when one considers the rain from the sky and cracking of earth?

87. Purification of the Heart and Success

Purification of the Heart and Success

For sure, success is achieved
By purifying the heart

For sure, success is achieved
By chanting, glorifying and appreciating your Merciful, Caring and
    Generous Rabb
For sure, success is achieved
By offering the daily prayers

But,
You prefer this worldly temporal life,
While
Afterlife is much better and permanent.

And even for sure,
This teaching was written in the previous scriptures
In the script of Abraham
And
In the script of Moses, the Torah
[87:14–19]

Discussion Questions

1. How does one attain success by purifying one's heart according
   to the above verses?
2. What is the method of purifying one's heart in the above verses?

88.   Reminder

So,
Remind them,
You are only a reminder
You are not over them a compeller or a controller.

After this,
Who turns away and does not recognize the Creator
Will have the greatest accountability by the Creator

For Sure, to Us is their return.
Then,
For sure,
Upon Us is their account.
[88:21–26]

Discussion Questions

1.   What is the position of messengers, prophets, or Muslims in the task of preaching and giving advice to others?
2.   What is the ideal method of advice in Islam?

89. The Happy Self

The Satisfied and Happy Self

Oh satisfied, content and happy self!
Come back to your Merciful and Forgiving Rabb
You will be satisfied, content and happy; because
Your Appreciative and Forgiving Allah is pleased with you for your
 good effort in the world,

After this, Allah will invite them and say:
"Enter among My special worshippers and
Enter My Heaven."
[89:28–30]

Commentary

In the above portion of the chapter, the self or the soul is pleased and
Allah سبحانه وتعالى is pleased. According to Muslims, the ultimate goal
in this world is to perform all the spiritual struggles to please Allah
سبحانه وتعالى. If Allah سبحانه وتعالى is pleased, the person will be happy,
content, and peaceful in this world and in the afterlife. Heaven is not the
fundamental goal but is given as a reward.

Humbleness or humility is the key in the spiritual journeys of struggle.
Especially, humbleness in the relationship with the Divine is the key. It
is not humiliating for Muslims to humble themselves in front of their
Creator. It is actually a desired state of elevation. Therefore, the word
A'bd in this chapter, translated to English, has different meanings, such
as worshipper, creation, servant, or slave. If the translations are taken
literally it can have a wrong contextual meaning in our current social
norms. In one's relationship with Allah سبحانه وتعالى, being a worshipper,
servant, and creation of the Divine is an honor but worshipping
and being slave to all the other beings is a dishonor according to the
understandings of Muslims.

Discussion Question

1. How can one reach the level of content self in life according to
 the teachings of Islam?

90.   Two Eyes, Two Ears, and One Tongue

Two Eyes, Two Ears, and One Tongue

Does the person think that no one sees them?
Didn't We give this person
Two eyes

Didn't We give this person
One tongue

Didn't We give this person
Two ears

Didn't We show this person
Two ways:
The truth and the real
The false and the deception
[90:7–10]

Discussion Question

1.   How should different arrangement of the body parts inspire the person according to the above verse?

91.   Success and Failure of the Self

Success and Failure of the Self

By the sun and its emerging brightness and
By the moon when it reflects the sun
By the day when it displays with the sun and
By the night when it covers the sun and

By the sky and the One who built it, and
By the earth and the One who expanded it
By the self and the One who perfected it
Then, the One who
Gave the person the choice of
Evil and the immoral or the good and the piety

After all this,
Certainly and for Sure,
Success and happiness is in the
Physical and Spiritual Purification of the self
Failure and depression is in the
Pollution, sinful, and evil command of the self
[91:1–10]

Discussion Question

1. How can the success and failure of the self be attained according
    to the above verse?

Right of an Animal

The Prophet of Allah said to them:
"Be careful of the Creator's camel and let her drink from the water."

But they rejected the Prophet, (did not care about his advice) and
    killed her,
So their Just Rabb sent a severe punishment upon them
Because of their evil,
And applied justice
Without any fear of its consequence
[91:13–15]

Commentary

According to the above verse, there were some arrogant people who demanded a miracle from Allah سبحانه وتعالى. Allah سبحانه وتعالى sent them a camel miraculously and they accepted it as a miracle. One day, while this camel was drinking water from the well, these conceited people killed this camel for no reason but to challenge Allah سبحانه وتعالى and their prophet. Due to this oppression, Allah سبحانه وتعالى sent a punishment and applied justice.

Discussion Questions

1. What are the animal rights in Islam?
2. Does a human hesitate from its consequence when applying justice?

92.   The Night

The Night

When the night covers
When the day rises
When Allah creates males and females
For sure,
 At the end, your efforts are diverse

The ones who are generous and charitable
And have respect for Allah
And acknowledge and testify the beauty of all signs from Allah
Then, we make everything easy for them

The ones who always hold back
And have arrogance
And deny the beauty of all signs from Allah
Then, We make everything difficult for them
[92:1–10]

Discussion Questions

1. If one recognizes Allah سبحانه وتعالى, how can things become easy?
2. If one does not recognize Allah سبحانه وتعالى, how can things become difficult?

93.   What Is after Will Be Better

What Is after Will Be Better[92]

In the morning hours,
In the night when it covers
Your Caring Rabb did not leave you
and
Your Loving Rabb does not hate you

What is after will be better
From before
Your Generous Rabb will give you so much that
You will be pleased and satisfied

Didn't Allah find you orphaned
and give you shelter

Didn't Allah find you lost[93]
and guide you

Didn't Allah find you in hunger and in need
and provide for you

Therefore,
Do not oppress an orphan
And,
Do not turn down a person in need

Therefore, after all this,
Appreciate and Pronounce constantly
all the favors of Your Generous and Loving Rabb
[93:1–11]

---

92. Inspired from M. Sells, "Selected passages of the Quran."[70]
93. Everyone is lost in reference to their prior times of not knowing and worshipping Allah in a true and genuine way. Therefore, the word "lost" is true for everyone at different levels. The word "lost" is not an accepted appropriate word if it is used for the Rasulullah ﷺ according to the traditional Islamic understanding. The Prophet was guided by Allah from his birth until his demise.

Discussion Questions

1. What is the significance of the above chapter in a Muslim practice?

2. What is the teaching of the above verse in one's relationship with Allah سبحانه وتعالى when the person encounters the evil in life?

94.   Open Chest

Open Chest

Didn't We open and expand your chest for you
So that you are in the state of peace and tranquility

And didn't We remove your burden,
Stress, and fear from you
Such a burden was
Cracking your back

After this,
Indeed, We increased your remembrance, and a good reputation of you

Remember!
Therefore,
For sure, with every hardship comes ease
For sure, with every hardship comes ease

Therefore,
When you have free time hold tight and don't waste it
But,
Indeed,
Turn fully to your only Merciful and Loving Rabb with desire and
Establish a sweet relationship

[94:1–8]

Commentary

There are certain chapters and verses in the Quran that are read for both ritualistic and talismanic purposes in everyday practice. This above chapter in its original language can be read for depression, physical and spiritual heart problems, anxiety, and sadness by some Muslims. A Muslim can read this chapter over and over until one's heart and emotions calm down according to some practices. The green transliterated text from Arabic is presented to allude to the original sounds with the experiential meanings in practice.

Discussion Questions

1. Is there a difficulty and easy cycle in life? Is this a religious teaching?
2. Do the people have lives filled with difficulties? Do the people have lives of ease?
3. Do the people read this chapter to treat any type of physical sickness?

95.   Perfection in Human's Creation

© Orla/Shutterstock.com

Perfection in Human's Creation

Certainly,
We created each human with the best composition of
Both physical and spiritual perfection
[95:4]

Commentary

According to the above verse, the composition of a human body is perfect: upright, symmetrical, and balanced in form and nature. According to the Islamic Scholars, for example, if one wants to put the eyes anywhere in the body other than its current location, then one can realize that its present location is perfect. The position of the hands is perfect. The spiritual faculties of a human are perfect and decode everything in the creation intrinsically. It is the free will of the person to continue in this bodily and spiritual perfection by recognizing and appreciating the Creator and fulfilling the Divine orders accordingly. Alternatively, using one's physical and spiritual faculties is the choice of the person when committing evil.

Discussion Question

1.   According to the remaining parts of the chapter, how can one oscillate between perfection and imperfection?

96.   Read, think, and learn!

© A. and I. Kruk/Shutterstock.com

Read, think, and learn!

With the name of your Nourishing and Caregiving Rabb, who created
    everything
Created the person from an embryonic cell

After this,

Read, think and learn!
Your Caring Rabb is the Most Generous and Gracious
The One who taught the abilities of learning and writing, the use of the
    pen
Taught the person what they did not know

After all this,
For sure,
This person becomes arrogant and self-deceitful
Thinking themselves free of need
Thinking themselves self-sufficient

Don't Worry!
Surely and Certainly
To your Just and Merciful Rabb is the return.
[96:1–8]

Commentary

This chapter is the very first verse of the Quran revealed to the Prophet. Since these verses were the initial revelation in the Quran, the scholars emphasize the importance of learning, education, and critical thinking that Allah سبحانه وتعالى teaches to all humans in understanding the religion and its relationship with all sciences.

Discussion Questions

1. How is the historical revelation of these verses in the Quran?
2. Why is the first command of Allah سبحانه وتعالى "Read" according to the scholars?

97.   The Night of Power

The Night of Power

Indeed,
We revealed the Quran in the night of power, and
Do you know what the night of the power is?
The night of power is better than one thousand months
In this night descends many angels and Gabriel on the earth
With the permission of their Merciful and Forgiving Rabb
Everywhere and every instant
Is in peace this night
Continues till the beginning of dawn
[97:1–5]

Commentary

This night has a special value in Muslim practice. It is the one night in the entire year that Allah سبحانه وتعالى sends special blessings on the earth for all the creation. With the suggestion of the Prophet, it is believed and practiced that this night is hidden in the last ten nights of Ramadan.

Discussion Questions

1. Why is this night better than one thousand months according to the practice?
2. Why is the date of this night not known according to the Muslim scholars?

98.   What is the correct and true religion for Christians and Jews?

What is the correct and true religion for Christians and Jews?

With the name of Allah, the All-Merciful, the Very-Merciful,
The People of the Book,
Christians, and Jews
Were not ordered except:
To worship only One Allah sincerely
As this has always been the correct religion of Allah[94]
Worshipping no one, but only One Creator

And, after this very first pillar
Establishing and Continuing to pray
Daily and regularly
And, at the same time
Sharing what were given to them: wealth, knowledge, and kindness

Certainly,
This has been always the correct and true religion.
[98:5]

Discussion Questions

1.   How do you interpret the correct and true religion definition?
2.   Why are the Christians and Jews especially addressed in the above verse?
3.   According to the verses of the Quran, why do the Christians and Jews have double reward from Allah سبحانه وتعالى when they become Muslims compared to the Muslims who were born in Muslim families?

---

94. Rendering for "lahuddiin"

99.   Atom's Weight of Good or Evil

Atom's Weight of Good or Evil

After death,
That Day,
People appear in groups
To be shown the reality of their actions

So that,
Who has an atom's weight of good
Will receive its reward

Who has an atom's weight of evil and oppression
Will face its accountability
[99:6–8]

Discussion Question

1.   What is the accountability after death in Islam?

100.   Self-Witnessing the Ungratefulness

Self-Witnessing the Ungratefulness

For sure,
The human being is unappreciative with their
Real Care-Giving and Sustaining Rabb

And
But for sure,
This person knows their ungrateful behavior
As a fact and as a self-witness
[100:6–7]

Discussion Question

1. How can one witness his or her unappreciative behavior in one's
   relationship with Allah سبحانه وتعالى؟

101.   Mercy and Justice of Allah

After all,
For sure,
The ones whose scale is heavy of good deeds
Will be in the best life after death with the mercy of Allah
The ones whose scale is light of good deeds
Will be engulfed by an abyss with justice
Due to what this person deserves
[101:6–9]

Discussion Question

1. How does the justice and mercy of Allah سبحانه وتعالى work in this world and afterlife in Islam?

102.   Knowing with Certainty

Boasting with your numbers: wealth, children, and degrees
Till you go down into your graves

Indeed, you will soon know the truth
Definitely, you will soon know the truth

Indeed, if you know the truth with knowledge
Then, you would understand the accountability, reward and
  punishment
Then, you will understand and realize everything with certainty
That, for sure, you will be questioned about everything at the end.
[102:1–8]

Discussion Questions

1.   What are the levels of knowing?
2.   Do the people boast with their bachelors, masters, PhD, or MD degrees? Do they have significance when the person dies according to this chapter?

103.   Importance of Time

Importance of Time

Certainly,
The time passes but
The person is in loss
Except the ones
who are in submission and surrender to their one and only Allah and
who do always the good and ethical action and
who remind each other of reality and
who remind each other of patience.
[103:1–3]

Discussion Questions

1. What do you understand from this chapter?
2. Why does "and" come instead of "or" for the definition of the ones who are not in loss?
3. Why do people feel anxious as they age and get close to death? What is the significance of time?
4. When do people need patience? How do people remind each other about patience?

104.   Slanderer and the Mean Person

Slanderer and the Mean Person

In the loss are every
Slanderer,
Fault-finder
Mocker,
Backbiter,
The mean person
The one relentlessly collects, stocks, and counts all his or her wealth
Thinking that this wealth will not last with the death
[104:1–3]

Discussion Question

1. According to the chapter above, why are slanderer, fault-finder, mocker, backbiter, and the mean person in loss? What does "in loss" mean in the above verse?

105.   Holy Sites and Invalidation of the Evil Plans by Allah

Did you see
How your Protecting and Preserving Rabb, dealt with the people
    coming for destruction with the elephants?
Did you see
how Allah invalidated their evil plans?
[105:1–2]

Discussion Questions

1. What is the incident of elephants in the history of Kabah?
2. How do Muslim scholars interpret the protection of the holy
    sites according to this chapter?

106.   Holy Sites and Safety

© Arden_Panikk/Shutterstock.com

Holy Sites and Safety

So that the holy sites, the Kabah, served by Quraysh can remain safe
Safe in their times of winter and summer
So that everyone can come, visit, worship and do pilgrimage
To this Holy House of the Protecting and Providing Rabb, the Kabah
Who made it worry free of hunger, fear and danger
[106:1–4]

Discussion Questions

1. How do you connect this chapter with the previous one?
2. What has been the current geographical, weather, and financial condition of Makkah where the holy sites are located?
3. Did the holy sites, Kabah, face any destruction and turmoil in their history?
4. What is expected with the destruction of Kabah in the prophecy of the Rasulullah ﷺ?
5. Do Muslims worship Kabah?
6. What is the significance of Kabah compared to human life in Islamic theology?

107.   Being Mindful in Chants and Prayers

Being Mindful in Chants and Prayers

In loss are the chanters, meditators, and worshippers
Who are not mindful, attentive and focused in their engagement
[107:4–5]

Discussion Questions

1. Is it difficult to fully focus during the meditation, chants, and worship? What makes it easy or difficult?
2. Does a prayer without full focus have benefits to the person? Why?

108.   The River and Expiration

Indeed, we have given you the river of Kowthar with no expiration
Therefore, appreciate, pray and worship to your Merciful and Caring
Allah
And do your sacrifice for your Most-Greatful and Praiseworthy Rabb
only

Don't worry about the ones who hate and cause problems for you
Indeed, your hater is the one who is unproductive, self-destructive, and
expired
[108:1–3]

Discussion Questions

1. If there are people who hate or cause problems for a person,
    what is suggested according to the above lines?
2. Is it easy to ignore the ones who cause trouble for the person?
    What makes it easier to ignore them?
3. According to the above verse, do the haters hurt themselves?
    Why and how?

109.   Dialogue, Tolerance, and Acceptance

Dialogue, Tolerance, Acceptance

Say: Oh the ones who do not recognize and accept Allah!
I do not worship and believe in yours and
You do not worship and believe in mine

And You do not worship and believe in mine
And I do not worship and believe in yours and

Your belief and worship is yours and
My belief and worship is mine
[109:1–6]

Commentary

This chapter establishes a ground for dialogue, tolerance, and acceptance for different people with different beliefs in a society. People can have differences. Although one does not have the same way of norms, having respect for each other is critical.

Discussion Question

1. Do the Muslim societies practice this notion of dialogue, tolerance, and acceptance today? How did they understand this in the past?

110.   Victory and Humbleness

Victory and Humbleness

When the help of Allah and victory comes
When you see people recognizing their Care Giver, Allah
Becoming content in their relationship with Allah and
Accepting the true message in abundance

Then, glorify your Real Doer and the Real Cause, your Sustaining Rabb
With full appreciation and full merit and
Increase in abundance your repentance to your Most Merciful Allah
Indeed, Allah is very and always Forgiving
[110:1–3]

Commentary

This chapter urges the believers to remember, glorify, and repent to
Allah سبحانه وتعالى in the times of personal or group achievements when
achieving a good cause. The lines urge the person to ask repentance in
the case of good cause due to possibilities of arrogance.

Discussion Question

1. How do you understand the above verse? Does a person
   become arrogant after an achievement? How can one prevent
   self-arrogance in this case?

111. Plot and Evil

Plotting and Evil

His wealth, and his struggle for plotting evil
Did not benefit him
[111:2]

Commentary

This short chapter is interesting. It talks about some family members of the Prophet and how they wanted to plot against him to harm and do evil to him. The only reason for their anger was the Prophet's message of inviting people believing in one Allah سبحانه وتعالى and discouraging them not to worship to the idols as their Creator. The chapter discusses the attitude of one of the uncles of the Prophet. He was so happy with Muhammad صلى الله عليه وسلم as his nephew before the prophethood. As soon as the Prophet started inviting people for believing in one Allah سبحانه وتعالى, his uncle viewed the Prophet, his nephew, as his chief enemy and started plotting against him.

Discussion Questions

1. Do the family members disown the person when this person changes his or her faith? Is it challenging for a person to face pressure from family members in this change?
2. Is it common for the people to have close family members plotting against the person? Why?

112.   Who is Allah?

Chapter of Sincerity and Unity

Say:

Allah is One.

Allah does not need anything or anyone but everything and everyone
    needs Allah.

Allah does neither have any parents nor any children.

Allah is Unique, not like any human, not like any creation.

There is no equivalent to Allah

[112:1–4]

Transliteration from the original scripture:

Qul Huwa Allahu Ahad. Allahu Assamad. Lam Yalid wa lam yuulad.
    Wa lam yakun lahu kufuwan Ahad.

Commentary

One of the key chapters in the Quran is the chapter of sincerity/unity
(Ikhlas). It is a key chapter in establishing a Union with the person and
Allah سبحانه وتعالى. Muslims rationalize, experience, and vocalize this
chapter in their prayers. They especially expand the understanding of
the key expression "La ilaha illa Allah." According to the Rasulullah
ﷺ, this one-line chapter has a value for Allah سبحانه وتعالى almost
equivalent to one-third of the full scripture of the Quran. The reason is
that this chapter presents the essence of Allah سبحانه وتعالى. Therefore,
the Prophet recommends this chapter along with the last two chapters
of the Quran to read them three times, blow into the hands, and wipe
the hands to the whole body for protection and blessing. This Quranic
chapter also has two unique names of Allah سبحانه وتعالى: Samad and
Ahad. Samad is a term only used for Allah سبحانه وتعالى. It does not have
any popular usage in the language. It generally translates as the One who
does not need anything, but everyone and everything needs Allah سبحانه
وتعالى. It is also interesting to note that Samadhi as a word is one of
the last stages that is attained in Hinduism, Buddhism, and Jainismand
Sikhism. In Islam, a person could be denoted as a servant of the Samad.[95]

---

95. As Abdussamad in Ar and it can be used as a name of a person.

Discussion Questions

1. What is the significance of this chapter in Islamic creed?
2. Why is this chapter named as the chapter of unity, or chapter of sincerity?
3. What is the suggested times of reading this chapter according to the practice of the Rasulullah ﷺ?

113.   Day

Day

Chant, Meditate and Say![96]

I take shelter
In my Protective, Watchful Rabb the Merciful Creator and Watcher of
the Day

I take shelter
In my Protective, Watchful Rabb from the harm of all the creations
that Allah creates

I take shelter
In my Protective, Watchful Rabb from the harm when night covers
with its darkness

I take shelter
In my Protective, Watchful Rabb from the harm of the self and the
persons indulging in evil talismanic powers and black magic[97]

I take shelter
In my Protective, Watchful Rabb from the harm of persons indulging
in jealousy and hatred
[113:1–5]

Discussion Questions

1.   Why is there a detailed description of taking shelter or protection
     from the evil?
2.   When do people read this chapter in practice?
3.   How many times should a person read this chapter for protection
     according to the teaching of the Prophet?

---

96. Qul translated as chant, meditate, and say instead of "say" as in literal translations in order
to reflect the practiced meanings.
97. Classical translations prefer to use magic which was avoided here. Magic in everyday
American language is mostly used to imply something positive rather than its literal meaning.

114.   Full Protection

Full Protection

Chant, Meditate and Say!

I ask protection and take shelter
      In Allah, the Merciful Creator of the people

I ask protection and take shelter
      In the True Authority of the people

I ask protection and take shelter
      In the True Deity of the people

I ask protection and take shelter
In the Merciful Creator, True Authority and True Deity
from all the temptations, and bad thoughts of evildoers
who constantly send evil thoughts and depressions to the chest of the
      people

I ask protection and take shelter
In the Merciful Creator, True Authority and True Deity
from all the evil of unseen beings, Jinn and humans
[114:1–6]

Discussion Questions

   1.   What is the significance of this chapter in practice?
   2.   Why is it critical to ask protection constantly in practice?

PART 3
PREFERRED METHODOLOGY OF TRANSLATION

Most people who practice Islam do not understand Quranic Arabic and rely on colloquial translations of the sacred text. In the English-speaking world, a contemporary translation of a particular passage can have a major impact on behavior and can even encourage social conflict. Each translation has different connotations in the target language. The goal is to minimize the connotations that are not suggested in the original text.

I argue that it is important to include the concerns of contemporary translation methods in the Quranic translations. As an example of this effort, an article on the method of translation of the verses of the Quran by Kumek[36] is presented in the Appendix. In this study, the preferred methodology of translation is to focus on the pragmatic method of Chesterman's[37] taxonomy that would prevail the exegetical meanings in translation. As an example of this preferred methodology for the Quranic verses, the study in the Appendix first reviews the existing popular translations of the verse in the Quran [3:64], often translated, as "a common word among us," then explores the traditional and contemporary exegetical meanings, and finally offers possibilities in translation. The "common word" verse is selected as an example for the analysis, because this verse has recently gained much public attention in the West for contemporizing the relationships between Muslims, Christians, Jews, and other religions.[38] After reviewing this methodology, one can realize that this book uses this preferred methodology in the selected passages from the Quran as presented in the Appendix.

APPENDIX

PERILS OF TRANSLATION:
TEXT AND BEHAVIOR
"A COMMON WORD AMONG US"
IN THE QURAN [3:64]

Preferred Methodology of Translation

Most people who practice Islam do not understand Quranic Arabic and rely on colloquial translations of the sacred text. In the English-speaking world, a contemporary translation of a particular passage can have a major impact on behavior and can even encourage social conflict. I argue that it is important to include the concerns of contemporary translation methods in the Quranic translations. In this study, I try to focus on the pragmatic method of Chesterman's [37] taxonomy that would prevail the exegetical meanings in translation. As an example of this effort, the current article first reviews the existing popular translations of the verse in the Quran [3:64], often translated, as "a common word among us," then explores the traditional and contemporary exegetical meanings, and finally offers possibilities in translation. This verse has recently gained much public attention in the West for contemporizing the relationships between Muslims, Christians, Jews, and other religions.

Introduction

This chapter is an effort to describe how sacred text can affect behavior in translations. I argue that exegetical translation is vital to reflect the original philological meanings from the source language (SL) of Arabic to the target language (TL) of English. That does not mean that the literal meaning of the verse is not important. The ideal Quranic translation, I think, should prioritize the contextual and philological motifs in the meaning along with semantic and syntactic concerns. Therefore, I will use the words contextual, interpretive, or pragmatic strategies[37] interchangeably in this article to assert the importance of prioritizing and conveying the "message" in the Quranic translations through exegetical meanings.

Recently, there has been considerable attention to the Quranic verses[42] relevant to contemporary social conflicts. Some scholars claim that particular verses in translations in the English-speaking world promote social conflict and even violence.[43] But many other commentators stress contextual understanding of the verses.[44] I fully agree that context and the meaning is crucially important in understanding scriptures, especially through pragmatic methods,[37] and this is one of my main arguments in this study; however, I want to untangle another, often untouched, problem in the current literature as well. This is the syntactic and semantic analysis of the English words and phrases chosen in translating the text from the source language of Arabic in order to understand their potential relationship to social conflicts, opposed to unity. Many people who practice Islam do not understand Quranic Arabic but rely on colloquial translations. An incorrect single translated word could divert the reader from the hermeneutical meanings.

As a methodology, I will analyze the available and popular English translations of one of the critical verses in the Quran, named or popularized as "common word." I will review the meanings from the contemporary and traditional exegesis in the literature. Finally, I will present the possible glitches of these available translations and offer possibilities of translations reflecting the equivalence from the source language of Arabic into a contemporary colloquial English. This may offer an alternative that captures unity rather than submerging in verbiage that suggests its opposite.

Translation Theories and the Quran

The purpose of this article is not a substantial indulgence with the translation theories and how it applies to Quranic Arabic. Rather, it is to casually explore and analyze a case of scriptural text (verse) from the source language (SL) of Arabic into the target language (TL) of English by reviewing some of the current available literature. In this perspective, I do not use a top-down approach of using the translation taxonomies and applying it to the text. Rather, I review and assume that current available widely popular translated texts into the target language already has value through text to genre then to discourse then to register which implies rhetorical purpose, communicative event, ideology/ perspective, and situationality respectively.[45] Chesterman's[37] taxonomy has already been used to review some of the Quranic divine names to explore some of the translation renderings.[46] Chesterman's translation model has two main groups: comprehension and production strategies. Comprehension strategy uses the examination of source language and full design of translation methods. Production strategy uses the results of comprehension design to transform the text from source to target language. This article uses the production strategy in the methodology of translation of scriptural text. I attempt to use a heuristic approach of translation classification in including three primary groups of production strategy: syntactic/grammatical, semantic, and pragmatic.[37]

SYNTACTIC	SEMANTIC	PRAGMATIC
Literal translation	Synonym	Cultural Filtering
Loan	Antonym	Explicitness
Transposition	Hyponym	Information Change
Unit Shift	Converse	Interpersonal Change
Phrase Structure Change	Abstraction	Illocutionary Change
Clause Structure Change	Distribution	Coherence Change
Sentence Structure Change	Emphasis Change	Partial Translation
Cohesion Change	Paraphrase	Visibility Change
Level Shift		Transediting
Scheme Change		Other Pragramatic Changes

Table 1   Chesterman's (1997) Production Strategies

Below is an outline of the concrete approach of the above three categories.

> If syntactic strategies manipulate form, and semantic strategies manipulate meaning, pragmatic strategies can be said to manipulate the message itself. These strategies are often the result of a translator's global decisions concerning the appropriate way to translate the text as a whole.[37]

In this perspective, I do not aim to nitpick much on syntactic and semantic issues, rather focus on pragmatic concerns or strategies of translation by bringing the conventional Quranic exegetical meanings into translation. In this perspective of reviewing the Quranic exegesis, the stance is translating this text to favor unity rather than discord among the religions. One of the key elements that I strongly believe and understand is the importance of cultural filtering in the taxonomy of pragmatic strategy in the table above by Chesterman[37]. If the naturalization, domestication, or adaptation of the source text is not adapted then exoticization, foreignization, or estrangement occurs.[47] Therefore, I frequently focus on cultural filtering (Chesterman) in the critique of the current translations and will offer possible alternatives.

Common Word

The "common word" in the verse of the Quran, [3:64], has attracted public and academic attention from not only Muslims but also from Christians and Jews. Yale Divinity School held a conference[42]. The Tony Blair Foundation[38] published a book on the topic. News articles appeared on NY Times[48] and BBC[49] focusing on this verse and the phrase "common word."

I argue that the translation of this text of the Quran in the chapter of Family of Imran shows a passage [3:64] calling to unity, a call often submerged in verbiage that suggests its opposite. The available translations of this passage into English seem to be different. These differences or deficiencies relate to the variances between Arabic and English in their syntax, semantics, and pragmatic translation strategies. [37] Translations inevitably leave some areas silent. Perforce, "translators are traitors," as the Italian proverb suggests and one can always argue the perspective of loss and gain in translations.[50] These silent connotations, as subtexts, still leave several possible interpretations. In English language, the preference for brevity excludes many possibilities that Quranic Arabic grammar permits and even requires. English favors the simplest narratives and leaves subtext areas dangling or silent. But, Arabic suggests multiplicities of allusions and possibilities of interpretation over the text. We need to look at the other contexts of these English words and what they suggest to current readers. In the West, this sort of Quranic analysis is still in an embryonic state.[51]

In this article, I try to center on the contextual exegetical meaning of the verse, *Kalimatin saaw āin baynan ā wa Baynakum,* "a common word among us," in the chapter of Family of Imran, verse 64, which calls Christians, Jews, Muslims, and other religions to a common ground. Analysis of the Quranic expressions—grammatical, idiomatic, metaphoric, stylistic, and contextual—can suggest dialogue among

Christians, Jews, and other religions[54]. One can say that the Quran in this verse urges people not to focus on doctrinal minutiae.

The portion of the verse focused upon in this article transliterates[91] as: *Qul! yā ahlul kitā[92] bi (kitaabi)[93] ! ta'alaw ilā kalimatin sawāin, baynanā wa baynakum, alla na'buda illa Allah, wa la nushrika bihi shayan, wa la yattqhizha ba'dunā ba'dan arbaban min dūni Allahi. Fain tawallaw, faqūlū: ashadū biannā muslimūn.*

The purpose of this article is not to suggest liberal expressions of the text of the Quranic verse but rather to review and interpret or translate the orthodox and linguistic approaches such as in the works of traditional scholars such as Al Jurjani,[94] or Zamahshari[95] to the language of contemporary time with the equivalence methodologies of translation as much as possible. Among the many factors of Quranic translation, morphological, epistemological, grammatical, idiomatic, metaphoric, stylistic, technical, and contextual (*urf*), apparent (*lafzi*) and hidden (*ishari*) meanings are important to distinguish.[52] In addition, there is a strong relationship between the translator and the translated text.

Mustansir Mir's literal analysis of the Quran, the Quran as literature[53][54] analyzes Quranic speech using linguistic concepts such as asyndeton, polysyndeton, parallelism, chiasmus, and "envelope." Toorawa[51] emphasizes the importance of showing an effort to conserve the original rhyme structure of the Quran when translated to English. Abu Zayd[55] in his article outlines the problem of sole literary approach to understand the message of the Quran.

---

91. Transliteration is a dictation or writing of the words from one language with different alphabet to another language through hearing. For example, one can encounter in writings "qul" or "kul" in transliteration of the same word, قل, from Arabic to English due to the expression of the similar sounds in English.

92. Arabic word structure requires correct elongation with each letter of a word. An incorrect more or less elongation of a letter for a word can change the meaning of it.

93. According to the widely-used Arabic transliteration scheme[56], to denote elongations in the transliterated text instead of writing kitābi, kitābi could be used.

94. Al Jurjani lived during the eleventh century. He was a famous Arabic linguistic specializing in Quranic eloquence, rhetoric, and metaphor.

95. Zamakshari was an Arabic linguist who lived between the eleventh and twelfth century. His book, *Al-Kashhaaf,* is one of the most famous Quranic linguistic commentaries.

Previous Translations and Their Glitches

Below are the different translations of the verse [3:64] in some of the most popular English interpreted Qurans. In the translation of Usmani,[96] the verse reads[3]:

> Say, O people of the Book, come to a word common between us and between you, that we worship none but Allah, that we associate nothing with Him and that some of us do not take others as lords instead of Allah. Then, should they turn back, say: "Bear witness that we are Muslims." [3:64]

This translation uses contemporary English including literal and exegetical meanings. I believe it misses idiomatic and metaphorical meanings; for example, using "turn back" instead of "turn away" for the meaning of rejection. "Turn back" suggests physically moving in the opposite direction whereas "turning away" suggests avoiding or rejecting an idea. Analyzing this translation through Chesterman's [37] taxonomy, phrase structure change in syntax leads to emphasis change in semantics and this leads to cultural filtering problem in pragmatic strategy of translation.

Yusuf Ali's[97][5] popular English translation, which also uses "turn back," reads:

> Say: "O People of the Book! Come to common terms as between us and you: That we worship none but Allah; that we associate no partners with him; that we erect not, from among ourselves, Lords and patrons other than Allah." If then they turn back, say ye: "Bear witness that we (at least) are Muslims (bowing to Allah's Will) [3:64].

Yusuf Ali's translation is one of the early English renderings, which makes it difficult for today's reader to understand the archaic language. Sometimes archaic language can cause abstraction in semantics.[37] This may lead to visibility change and explicitness in meaning.[37] This translation has the similar issue of the phrase "turn back" as mentioned above.

---

96. Mufti Taqi Usmani is a well-known legal Islamic scholar, born in Pakistan, who is closely working with the contemporary issues of Muslims, including those living in the West.
97. Yusuf Ali's English translation has been one of the first and most widespread one used in the West.

Arthur John Arberry[63] was a British Muslim journalist who worked at Cairo University as the department chair of Classics, translates[98] this verse [3:64], thus:

> Say: 'Oh! People of the Book! Come now to a word common between us and you, that we serve none but Allah, and that we associate not aught with Him, and do not some of us take others as lords, apart from Allah.' And if they turn their backs, say: 'Bear witness that we are Muslims.' [3:64]

Arberry's adaptation captures the meaning, but the language suffers from his coy archaisms like "aught with." He uses "turn their backs," implying hostility perhaps even greater than "turn back."

Saheeh International,[23] by a group of scholars in S. Arabia translate the verse as:

> Say, "O People of the Scripture, Come to a word that is equitable between us and you—that we will not worship except Allah and not associate anything with Him and not take one another as lords instead of Allah." But if they turn away, then say, "Bear witness that we are Muslims [submitting to Him]. [3:64]

The Saheeh International translation group comprises Western-born scholars. Although they understand the contextual meaning, using "turn away" instead of "turn back" in the above verse, they use a legalism such as "equitable" in the case of *sawāin* rather than a more inclusive phrase. "Equitable" is a legalistic term implying potential conflict and adjudication. Syntactically, this translation inclines to literal translation which may cause issues of cultural filtering and information change in pragmatic meaning[37].

Muhammad Pickthall was a Christian-born British Muslim thinker. Pickthall's translation[4], standard in the English world, reads:

---

98. The Quran is in Arabic. Islamic scholars do not consider the translations of the Quran as the original revealed text but close meanings with possible interpretations. Therefore, in Muslim tradition mere translation of the Quran is recommended with some commentaries. Thus, Pickthall's title is, for example, "The meanings of the glorious Quran." This could help the reader to understand the context and essence of the message.

Say: O People of the Scripture! Come to an agreement between
you and us: that we shall worship none but Allah, and that we
shall ascribe no partner unto Him, and that none of us shall
take others for lords beside Allah. And if they turn away, then
say: Bear witness that we are they who have surrendered (unto
Him). [3:64]

Muhammad Asad was a Jewish-born Austro-Hungarian Islamic thinker
who became Muslim in 1926 in Berlin. His translation reads[13]:

Say: O followers of earlier revelation! Come unto that tenet
which we and you hold in common: that we shall worship none
but Allah, and that we shall not ascribe divinity to aught beside
Him, and that we shall not take human beings for our lords
beside Allah." And if they turn away, then say: "Bear witness
that it is we who have surrendered ourselves unto Him" [3:64].

Due to the differences between English and Arabic, the choice of words
in translation is critical. Sometimes the wrong choice single word in
a verse could give unusual sub-textual meanings in English. This may
lead to major non-contextual interpretations of the entire verse. Both
Pickthall and Asad used a mixture of idiomatic and archaic styles, which
led to the problems of abstraction in semantics and lack of explicitness
in the pragmatic strategy of Chesterman's [37] categorization. However,
their apparent disadvantage for the American reader is their affinity for
the British style, such as preference of "shall" over present-day usages
of "will" or "should," depending on the meaning in American English.

Quranic Pragmatic Strategy

The Quran itself uses pragmatic strategies in different locations not
to convey a single message but to contextualize the meaning through
cultural filtering.[37] The Quran accepts the differences but emphasizes
the commonalities between these three religions, Islam, Christianity,
and Judaism. One of the main commonality is that each religion has
its own scripture from Allah سبحانه وتعالى. Muslims are holders of
the Quran. Jews are holders of the Tanach, which includes the Torah.

Christians are holders of the Bible. Quran urges its followers to establish
a common ground as "Peoples of the Book" among the religions with
divine scripture. "Peoples of the Book" in the orthodox exegesis of the
Quran includes Christians and Jews. The Quran asks Muslims, as the
followers of a divine scripture, to establish a common identity with
followers of different but kindred divine scriptures, such as Christians
and Jews.

Quranic figures of speech have commonalities with Biblical figures of
speech. In his article, Mir shows the distinctive features of Quranic
dialogue among different parties. Mir[53] says:

> There are, for example, no folk songs in the Quran, no elegies and
> lamentations, no prophetic rhapsodies, no idyllic poems, and
> certainly no acrostic. On the other hand, the Quran possesses a
> rich literary repertoire of its own. Besides making a masterful use
> of language on the level of words and phrases, it contains figures
> of speech, satire, and irony; employs a variety of narrative and
> dramatic techniques; and presents characters that, is (sic.) spite
> of the sparse personal detail provided about them, come across
> as vivid figures. For those who can read the Quran in Arabic, the
> all-pervading rhythm which, in conjunction with the sustained
> use of what may be called rhymed prose, creates in many Surahs
> a spellbinding effect that is impossible to reproduce. There is the
> characteristic terseness of the Quranic language which makes
> for some complex constructions, but which it is difficult to
> convey in English without being awkward. (52)

The Quran invites readers not to denounce unbelievers but to examine
them carefully[53]. The underlying assumption is that non-Muslims can
appreciate the merit, eloquence, and beauty of the Quran.

Mir divides Quranic dialogues into several types. Some are between
the prophets and the nation to which the message was sent. Others are
between Allah سبحانه وتعالى and prophets, or among humans both in the
world and the hereafter, or one-sided dialogues (monologues).

This paper suggests an additional dialogue in the Quran between
Muslims and People of the Book. This dialogue sometimes arises from

their questioning with the expression, y*asal ūnaka*. The phrase y*asal ūnaka* translates as "they are asking." Here, "they" are sometimes Jews, Christians, or Meccan pagans. Allah سبحانه وتعالى tells the Prophet Muhammad صلى الله عليه وسلم how to respond to them. Sometimes Allah سبحانه وتعالى reminds the Prophet Muhammad صلى الله عليه وسلم that there is a similar order in the Bible: the Gospel, the Psalms, and the Torah as in the Quran that they should follow. One of the obvious ones is that "killing an innocent human being is equivalent to killing all humanity" as mentioned in the Quran [5:32] and Talmud, in Mishnah Sanhedrin [4:5] and Babylonian Talmud Tractate Sanhedrin [37a]. Sometimes the Quran gives the response directly without entertaining the historical perspectives. For example, Jews in Madina ask about the nature of the soul or spirit (y*asal ūnaka anil ruh*…) and the response is that it is an "order from my Lord." [17:85] (i.e., Allah سبحانه وتعالى only knows it's real nature).

In the case of Surah Āl'i I'mrān,[99] in the verse [3:64]

> Say, O people of the Book, Come to a word common between us and between you (emphasis added by bolding the text), that we worship none but Allah, that we associate nothing with Him and that some of us do not take others as Lords instead of Allah. Then, should they turn back, say: "Bear witness that we are Muslims."[3]

Allah سبحانه وتعالى orders the Rasulullah ﷺ to be in communication with the other people of the Book, Christians and Jews. Allah سبحانه وتعالى also teaches the prophet and Muslims what the essence of the dialogue should be. The Quran suggests that a reminder and open communication that belief of the same Allah سبحانه وتعالى or the Creator should set the tone. This commonality should be the "common word" or belief shared before embarking upon further discourse.

---

99. Āl'i I'mrān is the name of the chapter of the Quran. Quran chapters are denoted either by the name of the chapter or by a number. This is the fourth chapter of the Quran that explains about Āl'i I'mrān. Āl'i I'mrān literally translates as the "Family of Imran." I'mrān is the father of Mary who is the mother of Jesus. Imran's wife makes a sincere prayer to Allah to have a child to dedicate him for Allah's path. As a result of this prayer, Allah gives her Mary. Mary, as a pious woman, dedicates her entire life worshipping Allah in the temple. According to the Quran, Allah gives Mary a son, Jesus, a Prophet of Allah and a Messiah.

Quranic language could be analyzed through meaning, grammar, idioms, metaphors, style, and context. For example, Quranic language uses different metaphors to depict certain occasions to picture vividly and lively a possible future and past panorama. Quranic grammar sometimes uses very complex structures, incorporating very rich stylistic language and dialogue. It deliberately chooses where to use active and passive tense, length of sentences (*itnāb*—explanatory sentences, *musāwi*—one-to-one correspondence, and *ijāz*—concise structure) and language registrars in syntactic and semantic strategies.[37]

Review and Analysis of the Exegetical Meanings

This section reviews and analyzes some of the traditional and contemporary exegetical meanings of this verse of the Quran in order to cognize the depiction of the idealized relationship of Muslims with other religions. The aim of this section is to ultimately represent these exegetical meanings of the verse in the translations. Fakhr al-Din al-Razi[57], a prominent medieval commentator and theologian, suggests three possible referents of the phrase *ahlul kitab*, "People of the Book." The first are the Christians of Najran, where the Prophet hosted them in his own mosque and encouraged them to perform their own Christian worship. The second possibility is the Jews of the Madina. The third possibility is both. Razi[57] emphasizes that the expression "people of the book" itself demonstrates respect for Christians and Jews. He says that it is a similar expression when someone makes a factual statement about another person. For example, a person is holding the entire Quran in his memory and he is called a *hafizul Quran*, "the holder of Quran" or "the memorizer of the Quran." The phrase "people of the book" is an honorific, like the phrase *hafizul quran* for a person who has memorized the Quran, a title of respect. In Muslim tradition, if someone is called *hafizul quran*, it is a dignified expression similar to calling someone Dr. (holds a degree of doctorate). This title is put in front of the person's name in all types of communication. Similarly, the Quran calls and teaches Muslims to address Christians and Jews or whoever received a book from Allah سبحانه وتعالى with an honorary salutation[57]. Especially in eastern cultures, honor and respect has a deeper meaning beyond its usage as a formal salutation.

Taʿalaw is a respectful phrase for gaining the listener's attention. *Kalimah* literally translated as "word" or a "statement" signifies a bridge between Muslims and "people of the book" according to Fakhr al-Din al-Razi.[57]

Sawāin could be literally translated as "common," "equal," and/or "share," and so forth. Fakhr al-Din al-Razi analyzes the word *insaf* from *nisf* (half) like *sawāin*. When something is equally shared into two halves (e.g., half for Muslims and the other share among the people of the book), bringing them together produces completeness and balance. [If only one owns half then it will be incomplete and possibly darkness and oppression.] Baghawi[100] (1987, first published circ. 1120) and other commentators especially emphasize the meaning of the *sawaun* as the judicial bond between us and them or the teachings that are common among different groups.

The Quran, with the expression *sawāin,* suggests that despite diverse ethno-religious labeling Jewish and Christian sacred texts and teachings have an essence, which they share with Islam.

This paper glosses *baynanā as* "among Muslims" in this verse. *Baynanā* is literally and contextually translated as "among Muslims" in this verse according to the normative exegesis of the Quran. This word implies that there could be a special education to implant this approach of commonality. On the other hand, *baynakum* is normatively translated as "Christians, Jews, Hindus, etc. . . ." This expression may refer to different religions through the agent of the scripture that was revealed.

The translation of the Quran by Yildirim,[44] suggests that the Quran invites Christians first because there are so many of them compared to followers of other religions. It invites all the other religions after. Yildirim says that the Quran shows how different races, religions, nations, or ethnic groups can agree and unite on common values, such as the legal right of freedom. M. Wahid Khan[58] comments that although the Quran criticizes the editorial deviations of the Old and New Testaments from the originals one can still incorporate the "commonality" of monotheism that serves as the ground for the unification. Some others[25] expand on this concept of commonality with the idea that we are all creatures but not inanimate like stones or soil. We are not

---

100. Baghawi is a prominent Islamic textual medieval commentator and theologian, d.1122.

plants. We are not lower animals. We are all humans. We share the same earth, air, water, food, and so forth. We have similar weaknesses and worries. We have the same Creator. So if this unity is one, then why do we concentrate on our minute differences?

According to Sabuni,[59] *sawāin* means *adl* in Arabic, which translates as justice. Reading this way, the Quran is calling all Christians, Jews, and Muslims to form a common ground, society, or a community on the basis of "Justice." Looking at the verses before and after this verse, this justice is first knowing Allah سبحانه وتعالى, His existence, uniqueness, and unity and building common grounds from there. Like Sabuni, Ibn Kathir (medieval expert on Quranic exegesis, died 1373)[60] glosses *sawāin* as *adl*, "justice" and "mercy," *nasf (ar.)*. Thus, *sawāin* connotes as justice, human rights, no superiority of one above another (*wal yattahizu ba'dunā ba'dan arbaba*), shared values, and unification under the umbrella of believing in one Creator. If one side has half and the other has nothing, the resulting imbalance is intrinsically unjust.

Through the recitational interpretation of the Quran, the Quranic words have internal rhythm (i.e., Musiki, Turk.) among the words. The letters that compose the word, the words that compose the sentences (verses), and the sentences that compose the chapters all have an internal rhythm and beat that either paint or echo (or both) the contextual meaning in the Quran. Even the sound of elongated words in the grammatical context is another point of emphasis. In Arabic, not all the words have elongation. *Sawāin* has an elongation (*mad*) in its recitation on the vowels of *ā* or "aa" according to recitation (*tajwēd*) rules of the Quran. In this verse, *sawāin*, "common," with the elongation in *ā* or "aa" suggests that there are a lot of commonalities. As an example, if we elongate the word a "lot" as if it reads in English as a "Loooot" of commonalities as does *sawaaaain* in its proper Arabic *tajwēd*. Elongation could imply the numerous or extended or many common values of Islam, Christianity, and Judaism.

The Quran stresses that accepting the monotheism must be voluntary, not forced as mentioned in the verse [2:256] "there is no compulsion (force) in the religion." In other words, it is illegal in Islamic law and tradition to force someone to change her/his religion. Therefore, if people don't accept the common ground of *sawāin* voluntarily, coercion is out of the question. People are free to choose what they want to believe and what they want to do.

The Quran repeats and highlights the concept of transgression or wrong (*zulm*). Transgression (wrong) comes in two types: one is against the Creator and the other is against the people. Transgression against the Creator does not bear any earthly accountability.[101] This transgression is mainly not recognizing Him as the Creator and consequently not appreciating His favors. The second type of transgression is against human dignity or social justice. It could involve invidious discrimination by race, ethnicity, or religion. The Quran suggests legal measures to eliminate this type of transgression. Some social Islamic scholars, such as Fazlur Rahman,[33] suggest that this law enforcement could be secular as long as the laws are fair, just, and, transparent which is the essential objective of the Quranic legal system (*sharia*).

As the result of both types of offenses, according to Quranic teachings, *wa lakinna anfusahum yazlimūn,* "the person in reality wrongs (oppresses or transgresses) himself." Therefore, in the later part of the verse discussed [3:64], after the invitation to a common word (the same Creator) the verse ends as "And if they turn away, say: 'Bear witness that we are Muslims.'" It reminds Muslims that if their invitation is not accepted or welcomed, one can tell them that we will still submit ourselves to our Lord's order.

The Core: Kalimah—A Word

In the remaining portion of the verse, the Quran instructs that there is a word, a value, or a theme for what Muslims, Christians, and Jews know and agree, *kalimah.* The Quran instructs that Christians, Muslims, and Jews all pledge to Allah سبحانه وتعالى to believe in Him and worship and please Him. As it says in Deuteronomy [6:4]: "Hear, O Israel: The Lord our Allah سبحانه وتعالى, the Lord is one." According to R. Marston

---

101. If the person does not believe in Allah this is a major transgression against the right of Allah in Islam. Transgression is due to not appreciating and recognizing the Creator. This type of transgression does not entail any type of punishment in the world. Therefore, according to the Islamic creed, one could see people who do not believe in Allah but may enjoy abundant bounties from Allah. Their transgression toward Allah will be addressed in the Hereafter. The punishment and reward will be in full effect over there.

Speight[61], Christ and his followers make the divine attribute of unity central to Christian theology. So this common word is with this recognition, accepting that no human is superior to another on religious grounds.

The basic common ground suggested by the Quran offers a way for humans to live together peacefully even though they may not share the same beliefs, practices, cultures, or ethnicities. A fundamental Quranic principle is that there is no compulsion in religion [2:255]. Muslims should build religious toleration by accommodating different faiths other their own [109:1-5]. This teaching provides a platform for people with different beliefs or unbelievers. Due to this teaching, non-Muslim ancient religions and communities were safe in Muslim lands, for example during the Abbasid, Umayyad, or Ottoman era, for centuries.

Many scholars explain the *kalimah* in the verse as the acceptance of one common Creator. The analogy could be that when there is a problem among the children, they go to their father to solve it for them. Similarly, the problems that humans face today could be solvable by the teachings of the Creator. There are common teachings in the sacred texts of the Creator. For example, stealing, lying, killing an innocent person, and backbiting are all sins in Judaism, Christianity, and Islam and also for most of the other religions. Being truthful, helping the poor and one's neighbors, and using good words are virtues in these religions. Taking a common Allah سبحانه وتعالى or Creator as the problem-solver suggests the ability and affinity to discuss social problems. As suggested,[62] practical implication of having the understanding of the common Allah سبحانه وتعالى between Jews, Christians, and Muslims could "move us all forward with common purpose, rather than act as a wedge that only drives us further apart." This could build avenues for potential solutions of the conflicts among these religions.

However, one may bring the question, for example, of abortion or other issues around which these three Abrahamic religions have similar teachings which modern secularists reject. The Quran emphasizes the personal free choice. Allah سبحانه وتعالى makes the best and just contextual and circumstantial judgment for His creation with His mercy according to the Quran.

In the Quranic understanding of *kalimah*, knowing Allah سبحانه وتعالى's name is not as important as correctly understanding His attributes. As mentioned in [17:110]: "Say: Call upon Allah سبحانه وتعالى, or call upon the Merciful (Ar-Rahman); whichever you call upon, to Him belong the Names Most Beautiful . . . " This may suggest that the Creator could be called Allah سبحانه وتعالى, Lord, Allah, Adonai, Elohim, Yahweh, Universal Intelligence, or Brahma[102] as long as it means or implies one of the beautiful and perfect names of the Creator.

Furthermore, in referring to the Creator, correct understanding Allah سبحانه وتعالى's and true attributes are essential according to the Quran. For example, the pagans during the time of the Rasulullah ﷺ called the Creator with the proper Islamic name, Allah. But, the monotheistic understanding of Allah سبحانه وتعالى was not there. Allah was one god among many. The Quran educates them by asking critical questions. It asks [23:84–85]: Say: "Whose is the earth, and who is in it, if you have knowledge?"[63] They say, Allah's سبحانه وتعالى). "Say: 'Will you not then remember?'" The Quran asks the pagans again [23:86–87]: "Say: who is the Lord of the seven heavens and the Lord of the mighty Throne? They say, Allah سبحانه وتعالى. Say: Will you not then be Allah-fearing?"[653] These questions are to lead idolaters to reflect on their understanding of Allah سبحانه وتعالى. The pagans believe in Allah سبحانه وتعالى (Creator) and at the same time, they believe in different idols as gods. Here, the Quranic style is pushing them to rethink their henotheism so that they do not associate any partners with Him. The common grounds could be expanded to commonalities such as love, ethics, and accountability.

The Quran urges people not to focus on doctrinal minutiae. The following verse of the Quran again in the Chapter of Family of Imran [3:65] gives Prophet Abraham عليه السلام as the example of practicing this common word although there is a dispute about the religion to which he belongs. The Quran emphasizes the importance of leaving this inessential argument of group "ownership" of Abraham عليه السلام.

---

102. In Islamic creed, correct understanding of the Creator with His proper name is Allah. All the best and beautiful names in its perfectness belong to Allah. These names and attributes of the Creator, Allah, are in the Quran and in the sayings of the Rasulullah ﷺ. There is a substantial opinion among the scholars of Islamic creed that calling or referring to Allah with the attributes and names other than the Quranic ones could be problematic.

Rather, it asks the followers of three religions to concentrate on the essence of his message of beliefs and values.

Finally, the Quran does not avoid demonstrating the differences of beliefs or values. It vividly contrasts the differences in multiple occasions. For example, in the immediate previous verses [3:59–63] right before the discussion of the verse of this article [3:64], it points out the difference of the belief between Christians and Muslims on Jesus. For example [3:59–60]:

> For (the Creator) Allah, Jesus's creation is similar to creation of Adam . (Adam was both without father and mother). Allah created Adam from mud, Allah said "Be" and Adam was created. The truth is from your Lord. You unquestionably should not have any doubt about it. (my trans.)

The above verse indicates that just as Allah سبحانه وتعالى created Adam عليه السلام without any father and mother, Allah سبحانه وتعالى certainly can create Jesus without any mother. Adam عليه السلام was not divine and so Jesus was not divine according to the Quran. But then, it directs or advises on a possible methodology that dialogue and communication start with common and shared values rather than pointing out these conflicts. The Quran then suggests that a possible source of dialogue among these three religions could be the values of Abraham عليه السلام. It shows a path in order not to be obstructed by mere ignorant "ownership" arguments among the followers of different religions about the teachings of Abraham عليه السلام. But, rather it suggests that the focus should be on the essence of his message that he symbolized straightforwardness and believing in one Allah سبحانه وتعالى.

One other possibility of Kalimah, the word, could be Jesus himself. This argument has a place in both Muslim and Christian resources.[64] When Jesus's miraculous birth and immaculate conception was explained in the Quran, Kalimah is used [4:171]. On the other hand, in Christian sources, word of Allah سبحانه وتعالى (logos) is a common approach to explain the birth of Jesus.[65] In this case, the meaning of the verse can emphasize the commonalities shared among Muslims and Christians could be Jesus and his teachings.

It seems irrational and unnatural, as some of the post and neo-orientalists assert,[43] to interpret obvious commonalities of Christianity, Judaism, and Islam as diverging points and not as common traits, since the obvious commonalities among all Abrahamic religions are very vivid and almost need no interpretation.[103]

Recently, some scholars[38] interpreted *kalimah*, "Common Word" as the "love of Allah سبحانه وتعالى" and "love of your neighbor." "Love your neighbor" interpretation included as all the humanity regardless of their faith or ethnic tradition. Jifri[38] mentions that Allah سبحانه وتعالى has sent books to solve human problems, but religions become part of the problem. According to him, Allah سبحانه وتعالى creates beauty, and humans love beauty; therefore, they should love Allah سبحانه وتعالى. Humans have a tendency to love the one who is benevolent. This type of love implies a natural love toward the Creator. People cannot generally choose their "neighbors." A person may change his house but how about his town, his city, country, or planet? Jifri[38] interprets this as the choice of Allah سبحانه وتعالى, that you should love your neighbor even though your neighbor may not be a pleasant person, as in the traditional Muslim example of the famous Jurist, Imam Abu Hanifa's relationship with his neighbor.[104] In a global scale, a person's neighbor may be of a different color, ethnicity, or religion. Understanding and interpreting this common word, *kalimah*, becomes more critical. Syed Husain Nasr (Volf[38]) summarizes the classical approaches and suggests similarities about the understanding of Allah سبحانه وتعالى, and its universal teachings among Islam, Christianity, and Judaism. He harshly criticizes

---

103. I think Crone[43] takes a deliberate stance to distance Christianity from Islam. Her analysis of the Quranic stories interestingly reads the commonalities as conflicts. It seems that she is not focusing on the literal text but commentaries.

104. Imam Abu Hanifa lived between 699 and 767. His legal teachings are popular in Muslim societies. He was also a devout worshipper of Allah. He had a neighbor who used to drink and sing loudly all night, disturbing Imam Abu Hanifa during his worship. Due to the strong emphasis to neighborly rights in Islamic jurisprudence, Abu Hanifa put up with his neighbor for many years. One day, he did not hear any noise from his neighbor and investigated the situation immediately. He found that the police had arrested him. He went to the police and bailed him out. As his neighbor witnessed this, he was perplexed and ashamed of himself and stopped drinking and became a pious disciple of Allah.

the teaching or vulgarization of a separate Allah [105]سبحانه وتعالى among Abrahamic عليه السلام traditions.

Some Sufis such as Rumi interpret the common word as any human being with any belief. Rumi[106] [66] illustrates this in his motif:

> Come, come, whoever you are.
> Wanderer, worshipper, lover of living, it doesn't matter
> Ours is not a caravan of despair.
> Come even if you have broken your vow a thousand times,
> Come, yet again, come, come (151).

Possibilities in Genres Reflected in Translations

After the above analysis, to emphasize the contextual insinuations or pragmatic methods,[37] I will present some possibilities of translations from SL to TL. I primarily use the cultural filtering method[37] by considering orthodox and contemporary exegetical meanings. Subsequently, I will review the possible different syntactic and semantic meanings of each word or phrase and insert it in the passage. The tags for each possible different passage will be Aa, Ab, Ac, Ba, and Bc. In these possible translations, the differences are compared to the main translation Aa. In each case, the whole verse is presented. It is purposeful to not only present the difference for the meanings. In normative scholarly and legal interpretations and exegesis of the Quran, contextual (*siyāq and sibāq*[107]) understandings of the verses are paramount.[67]

The phrase *qul,* "say," is used to mean to inform, communicate, notify, or to announce. Therefore, it will be more clear to use the verb inform as hyponym[108] in semantics[37] with its exegetical meaning although the

---

105. An Evangelist institute argued that Muslims and Christians have a separate Allah. Sayyid Hussain Nasr brings an example from Coptic Arab Christians in Egypt that they call Allah Allah, exactly the same as the Muslim phrase. Allah is the same word for the proper name of the Creator. The first verse of Genesis [1:1] in the Arabic Bible is "Allah created the heavens and the earth."
106. Jalal Ad-Din Rumi is a poet, theologian, and mystic scholar who lived in current Afghanistan, Iran, and Turkey between 1200–1273. His poems are translated to English and have gained universal popularity.
107. Siyāq and sibāq are terms to indicate the methodology in the Quranic exegesis for understanding the contextual meaning of the analyzed verse by examining the prior and following verses.
108. Hyponym ensures in semantics a specific meaning rather than a general meaning.

literal translation of *qul* is "say" as most of the translations preferred. "Say" means to utter words[68] in the colloquial English language. Here, the *siyāq and sibāq* in the Quranic exegesis suggest that *qul* does not have a "passive" stand of uttering words but rather informing and communicating with the other scripture followers. This is a very vivid example of cultural filtering in pragmatic strategy of translation.[37]

The expression *yā*, is a verbal exclamation mark, like "oh!" in English. One does not commonly and contemporarily use "oh!" unless in an informal conversation, as for example, "Oh My Allah سبحانه وتعالى." In the verse, Allah سبحانه وتعالى uses *yā*, "oh!" to focus attention on an important message. *Yā* could perhaps mean exegetically "please pay attention!" to something "astonishing" or "amazing" that follows. With the exegetical meanings, there is a unit shift of an exclamation to a phrase in syntax[37] and how this could be a cultural filtering issue from SL to TL.

Ahlal kitab literally translates as the people of the book. The connotation is that Allah سبحانه وتعالى revealed earlier scriptures so that the Rasulullah ﷺ and all Muslims recognize and accept them. In English, there is no phrase as "people of the Book" unless it is a Muslim audience. So, one can prefer to use hyponym and abstraction in semantics to translate this expression as "followers of earlier revelation."[13]

Taʾalaw literally translates as "come." In the verse, it implies calling parties together to resolve a dispute. It is an invitation to suggest a solution to an issue that could lead to puzzlement or argument as mentioned in the verses of the Quran [3:61], [3:64], [3:167], and [6:151]. Therefore, instead of using the literal translation, "Let's get together and discuss or realize," seems a better gloss which includes unit change in syntax; paraphrase, and emphasis change in semantics and cultural filtering and information change in pragmatic method of translation.[37]

Coming to the complex part of the discussion, *Kalimatin sawāin* is translated as "a common word" as presented below in translation "Aa," "a word common,"[3][63] "common terms,"[5] "a word that is equitable,"[23] "an agreement"[4], and "tenet which we and you hold in common."[13] In these renderings, some prefer to use literal translation, transposition, and unit shift in syntax; some use hyponym, emphasis change, and paraphrase in semantics, and some use cultural filtering, partial translation, and explicitness in pragmatic methodology.[37] *Kalimatin sawāin* is mentioned as a singular indefinite article (*nakirah*), which may imply the commonalities could be many and should be realized instead of having a definite article of *al kalimatu assawāu*. The remaining portion of the verse suggests, for this common word, realizing the common Creator and not to worship anything except Allah سبحانه وتعالى. Therefore, Yusuf Ali translated it as "common terms" in plural with the cultural filtering and replacing the general word, "term," with "values" as hyponym. Combining Ali's and Asad's translation, a possible translation for "kalimatin *sawāin*" is "values which we and you hold in common" as presented below in "Ac." Then, we clarify that in this commonness one of the significant one is "worshipping the same creator" by adding the expression "among" them as unit shift in syntax. Such glosses reflect the polysemy of a word like *kalimatin*. A word in English means "a single distinct meaningful element of speech,"[68] although *kalimatin* translates literally as "word." For the context of the passage of the verse [3:64], it holds the meanings of value and theme. Therefore, in different presentations of translations, I use for the translation of the word *kalimatin*, value or theme.

Sawāin stems from an Arabic root word and usually glosses as "justice" and "fairness." We can see this glossing in "Ab" presented below.

Translation "Aa" below is the closest literal translation that could be given with the exegetical meanings. I analyze the verse in three parts. The first part consists of Aa, Ab, Ac, Ba, and Bb, which have possible different translations of the same part of the verse. I treat the second part of the verse after the first part.

> Aa)
> Inform All Christians and Jews and other followers of a Scripture about this Amazing Fact!
> Please Pay Attention Followers of the Earlier Revelations!
> Let's get together and realize a common word between you and us.
> This common word is not to worship anything except our same and common Creator.

Ab)

Inform All Christians and Jews and other followers of a Scripture
about this Amazing Fact!

Please Pay Attention Followers of the Earlier Revelations!

Let's get together and realize a common *and just* theme between
you and us.

This common word is not to worship anything except our same
and common Creator.

Ac)

Inform All Christians and Jews and other followers of a Scripture
about this Amazing Fact!

Please Pay Attention Followers of the Earlier Revelations!

Let's get together and realize the values that we, and you hold
in common.

Among these values, primarily, is not to worship anything
except our same and common Creator.

Here, "Ac" is the preferred translation for our analysis when we combine
exegetical meanings.

If we abbreviate the translation of the verse it reads as: This common
word, value, or theme is that we worship the same Allah سبحانه وتعالى.
This common theme is that we only worship Allah سبحانه وتعالى. With
the more interpretive meanings the verse could possibly read: This
common value is the love of Allah سبحانه وتعالى. This common theme
is the justice.

In normative Quranic exegesis, the Rasulullah ﷺ is an agent to carry the
message from Allah سبحانه وتعالى to people like other messengers. Still,
in most of the phrases when Allah says in the Quran "Say" (Qul), the
addressee is actually all believers (Muslims). In other words, Muhammad
Iqbal stresses[69] that a person should read the Quran as if it was revealed
to the reader not to the Rasulullah ﷺ.

If we take into account cultural filtering in a pragmatic approach,[37] the verse reads as:

> Ba)
> A scripture from Allah to the Messenger:
> My dear Beloved Messenger Muhammad,
> Tell the Believers (Muslims)
> To Inform All Christians and Jews and other followers of a Scripture about this Amazing Fact!
> Please Pay Attention!
> Let's get together and realize common and just values among us.
> This common word among us is not to worship anything except our same and common Creator.

Another possible gloss emerges from the conventional and contemporary linguistic analysis of the words under discussion:

> Bb)
> A scripture from Allah to the Messenger:
> My dear Beloved Messenger Muhammad,
> Tell to the Believers (Muslims)
> To Inform all the Christians and Jews and other followers of a Scripture about this Amazing Fact!
> Please Pay Attention!
> Let's agree on the universal human values to live together on the earth peacefully.
> This common value among us is not to worship anything except our same and common Creator.

The second portion of the verse could continue in different translations as presented in Taqi Usmani's[3]:

> That we worship none but Allah, that we associate nothing with Him and that some of us do not take others as lords instead of Allah.

In Yusuf Ali's translation,[5]

> That we worship none but Allah; that we associate no partners with him; that we erect not, from among ourselves, lords and patrons other than Allah.

In Arberry's translation:

> That we serve none but Allah, and that we associate not aught with Him, and do not some of us take others as lords, apart from Allah.

In Saheeh International:

> That we will not worship except Allah and not associate anything with Him and not take one another as lords instead of Allah.

In Pickthall:

> That we shall worship none but Allah, and that we shall ascribe no partner unto Him, and that none of us shall take others for lords beside Allah.

Finally, in Asad's:

> That we shall worship none but Allah, and that we shall not ascribe divinity to aught beside Him, and that we shall not take human beings for our lords beside Allah.

All the translators above seem to be in agreement that the main notion is to realize and accept our common Creator, Allah سبحانه وتعالى. Then, the remaining part of the verse emphasizes the pure monotheism to explain what it means by a common Creator. The first condition is to accept only Allah سبحانه وتعالى as the Creator. It is to worship nothing but Allah سبحانه وتعالى. Some of the above translations use "partner." In English, the word "partnership" has generally positive or constructive meaning. Here, a negative or critical meaning is intended in the SL.

The first possible meaning is that a purposeful and explicit or implicit "division" or "split" in the pure belief in the one divine Creator is a conceivable problem. The second possible meaning is that assuming the words of other humans as the words of Allah سبحانه وتعالى is a problem. This could be implicit and mentioned later in the verse because people generally do not take other humans as their Lords, at least in our contemporary time, explicitly. One should remember that there were the cases of kings or pharaoh in the past who had the claims of having divine attributes. There is the emphasis that Allah سبحانه وتعالى does not have any coequals or partners. Neither can divine pharaohs or god kings compete with Allah's سبحانه وتعالى authority. Considering exegetical meanings, "except" is a better word in our TL of contemporary English as used in Saheeh International.

In the beginning of the verse, Allah سبحانه وتعالى calls different groups to make an agreement. Legal language ideally should have "shall," as used in the translations of Pickthall and Asad. "Shall" suggests both future and necessity. I think both Pickthall and Asad translations reflect British usage, in which "shall" is common as American English prefers "will." This brings the visibility change in TL for pragmatic methods.[37]

With the contextual (*siyāq-sibāq*) meaning each "waw" has different meanings. With this, the preferred translation for the portion of the verse could be:

> That we should not worship anything except Allah. This is because we should not ascribe any equal with Allah. And therefore, we should not consider human beings as divine. We believe that only Allah is divine.

Alternatively, by considering English language's preference for brevity, simplicity, and abstraction in semantics,[37] we could change the above first part of the verse as in the sentence below, as the TL still could have space for the meaning:

> That we worship only to Allah. This is because we should not ascribe any equal with Allah. And therefore, we should not consider human beings as divine. We believe that only Allah is divine.

Final and third part of the verse is, in Usmani:

> Then, should they turn back, say: "Bear witness that we are Muslims." [3:64]

Yusuf Ali glosses:

> If then they turn back, say ye: "Bear witness that we (at least) are Muslims (bowing to Allah's will)."

Arberry glosses:

> And if they turn their backs, say: "Bear witness that we are Muslims." [3:64]

In Saheeh International it is:

> But if they turn away, then say, "Bear witness that we are Muslims [submitting to Him]."

In Asad's translation:

> And if they turn away, then say: "Bear witness that it is we who have surrendered ourselves unto Him."

As I take the objective of cultural filtering and information change[37] through exegetical meanings, "Muslim" could not be in its literal meaning. If a person has all the qualities of believing and worshipping in one Allah سبحانه وتعالى purely and not making others as his or her Lord, then that person is a "Muslim" although they may not be literally called "Muslim." It seems likely that the verse does not intend the word "Muslim" to refer merely in its sectarian sense but to Bible reading monotheists in general, whether or not they subscribe to all the minutiae of Islamic orthodoxy. In this case, the word "Muslim" is a very clear example of translation and a possible problem is how it can capture a call to unity rather than submerging in verbiage that suggests its opposite. If the translator that takes the literal meaning, as most of the translators did in the current available English translations of the

Quran, then the meaning suggests the group identities of segregation or conflict. As explained above, when one really focuses on the contextual meaning one can clearly realize that the goal of this verse is to establish commonality and unity rather than forming group identities.

Here, "Tawalla" is used to mean "rejecting the message" as a unit shift in syntax. With these meanings, there is the message of conclusive approach of the communication, with the expression "Fain" meaning that "After all" as explicitness in pragmatic methodology.[37] On the other hand, "bear witness" is not a commonly used English phrase. "Be a witness" fits better in the TL as a way of phrase structure change in syntax. The audience is asked to testify that a speaker is accepting the message even if the audience does not accept it. With this in mind, a possible translation from ST to TL could be:

> After all, if they reject this message then tell them "Be our witness that we are accepting this message as Muslims do."

Or preferably with the exegetical meaning of monotheism for the word "Muslim," and the cultural filtering the translation in TL could be:

> After all, if they reject this message then tell them "Be our witness that we submit ourselves to one Allah."

Combining all the above analysis, the article glosses the verse this way:

> *Inform all Christians and Jews and other followers of a scripture about this amazing fact!*
> *Please pay attention followers of the earlier revelations!*
> *Let's get together and realize the values that you and we hold in common!*
> *Among these values, primarily, is:*
> *We worship only to Allah. We should not worship anything except our same and common Creator.[109]*
> *This is because; we should not ascribe any equal with Allah.*

---

109. The Arabic reader will note that "That we only worship to Allah" is inserted in the translation to give an exegetical complementary meaning to the following part "We should not worship anything except to our Same and Common Creator."

And therefore, we should not consider human beings as divine.
We believe that only Allah is divine.
After all, if they reject this message then tell them:
"Be our witness that we submit ourselves to one Allah"

This article has reviewed and analyzed different glosses to arrive at the above final version. There is a conventional method of meticulous microanalysis of sacred texts in Islam (i.e., usūl at-tafsīr or al-hadīth) which this article has not *fully* but maybe partially implemented in the examination of the studied verse. For example, in the full analysis of exegetical meanings (at-tafsīr), if the focus is to understand the expression, first the words of the expressions are analyzed linguistically. Then, the meanings of the verse are analyzed within the verse with the words coming before and after it. Then, the previous verses, *siyāq,* and the verses after, *sibāq,* are analyzed to understand the primary contextual meaning. Then, the chapters making up the verses are analyzed before and after that specific verse. There may be interpretations due to the location and time of the revelation of the verse. The "reason of revelation," *asbab nuzul,* is added in the interpretation. The same expressions in other parts of the Quran are analyzed to understand how the same expressions are used. The analyst draws upon the hadith literature for the same contextual meanings, the literature of Arab poetry, and writings for the additional possible meanings and the literature of classical exegesis for comparison (*qiyās*). Afterward, hermeneutical analysis continues by evaluating early interpretations by the companions (*sahabah*) of the Rasulullah ﷺ and the canonized understandings of the Quran among the famous jurists. Future researchers could address all these possibilities. The goal is to understand and give the possible meanings of the expression in the verse with a thorough overview of the literature within the framework of Islamic scholarship, and finally, translate these possible meanings amid the objective of equivalence from the source language of Arabic to the target language of English.

Concluding Remarks for the Preferred Methodology of Translation

Lay readers rarely have access to a scriptural scholar. Blame is habitually given to the monotheistic religions and their sacred texts for the conflicts that we face today. One can ask: What should we do in a world occupied with humans with different theologies, beliefs, cultural practices, physical appearances, and social norms? How do we establish a consensus that people with these differences are still to be respected, and can freely and peacefully live in a society together?

With the concern of reacting to these questions, this article has reviewed the English translations of the verse [3:64], many times referred to as the "common word verse," in the chapter of Imran (Father of Mary). Some of the available popular translations have differences in syntax, semantics, and pragmatic methodologies which may alter the meaning from SL to TL and form obscurity for the reader.

An emphasis on pragmatic translation[37] could accurately reflect the design embedded meanings in the Quranic verses. A lack of these sensibilities in the translation can promote conflict between theologies and groups that need to exist today.

For the purpose of the English reader, I believe that the pragmatic approach of translation optimizing the equivalence concerns in the methodology of translation is vital. It is possible that the translators may choose the similar syntactic and semantic approaches drawing upon each other's translations. Therefore, in the above-preferred translation of the verse, my effort has been combining the exegetical meanings to clarify for the reader in TL by primarily using the pragmatic approaches.[37] That does not mean that the syntactic and semantic meanings of the verse are not important. The ideal translation, I think, should prioritize the exegetical meanings through pragmatic methods.[37] Subsequently, the translator could have the concern of keeping the syntactic and semantic meanings and be concerned about the "internal rhythm" (eloquence) of the Quran in syntax and semantics by choosing proper words such as rhyming with the previous word or verse or giving the different meanings of awe, astonishment, or happiness or giving convoluted and deeper meanings with homonymy as in the text of the original Arabic revelation of the Quran that can complement all of them. Therefore, I sympathize with the translator when she/he realizes all these properties in the original text of the Quran but is not able to transfer them to the English language, especially when there is any case of a sacred text believed to be revealed from a Divine source.

EPILOGUE

The first part of this book is a brief introduction to Islam with questions and answers. The second part presents selected verses from each chapter of the Quran translated to English with their interpretive contextual meanings. The third part discusses methodology of the translation used in this book as the preferred methodology of translation of the Quran from the original language of revelation, Arabic to the present-day English. This part focuses on a case study of one verse and how this can be reflected in translation as a methodology.

In this book, some relevant verses of the Quran were selected based on social contexts, especially pertaining to Western readers. Muslim readers can benefit from this book by engaging different possibilities of discussion compared to their traditional education about the Quran.

The translations try to reflect the contemporary words rather than the traditional and archaic styles. The poetic style of the Quran is one of the difficult parts to reflect in the translation although there were some efforts in this book for some of the verses. To allude to this effort in this text, the color code with symmetry and rhythms are present.

Combining these three perspectives, this book can open different viewpoints especially for college readers and general readers with discussion questions.

Lastly, there are 114 chapters in the Quran. A thematic content of the selected verse is carried to the title with its original chapter number. One should not confuse this title with the normative accepted chapter names of the Quran as also presented later in this book. At least one verse is selected from each chapter of the Quran from 114 chapters. The section numbers denote the number of chapters. For verse selection of each chapter, the two numbers in brackets denote the chapter and verse numbers respectively.

Some chapters have more than one theme selection. There are more verses that could be selected from each chapter. The goal of this book is to introduce the new readers to the Noble and Honorable Quran with some selected verses.

Yunus (Jonah) Kumek, PhD
Lecturer on Muslim Ministry & Spiritual Care
Harvard Divinity School
Fall 2019

BIBLIOGRAPHY

[1]   Hackett, M. L. A. C. "Pew Research Center," 6 April 2017. http://
       www.pewresearch.org/fact-tank/2017/04/06/why-muslims-are-
       the-worlds-fastest-growing-religious-group/. Accessed 26 June
       2018.

[2]   Adamson, P. *Philosophy in the Islamic World*. Oxford University
       Press, 2016.

[3]   Usmani, T. *An Approach to the Quranic Sciences*. Adam
       Publishers, 2006.

[4]   Pickthall, M. W. E. *Holy Quran*. Kutub Khana Isha'at-ul-Islam,
       1977.

[5]   Ali, A. Y. *The meaning of the glorious Quran*. Islamic Books, 1938.

[6]   Hanbal, A. B. *Musnad Imam Ahmad Ibn Hanbal*. Dar-Us-Salam
       Publications, 2012.

[7]   Musaad, W. *Rihla 2018*. 3 July 2018.

[8]   Armstrong, K. *Muhammad: A Biography of the Prophet*. Phoenix,
       2001.

[9]   Ramadan, T. *In the Footsteps of The Prophet*. Oxford, 2007.

[10]   Al-Bukhari, M. *The Translation of the Meanings of Sahih
       Al-Bukhari*. Kazi Publications, 1986.

[11]   Siddiqui, A. *Sahih Muslim*. Peace Vision, 1972.

[12]   Cornell, V. *Voices of Islam*. Praeger Publishers, 2007.

[13]   Asad, M. *The Message of the Quran: Translated and Explained*.
       Al-Andalus Gibraltar, 1980.

[14]   Tarakci, M. & S. S. "The Quranic View of the Corruption of the
       Torah and the Gospels." *Islamic Quarterly*, vol. 49, no. 3, 2005,
       p. 227.

[15]   Ernst, C. W. *How to Read the Quran: A New Guide, with Select
       Translations*. The University of North Carolina Press, 2011.

[16]   As-Suyuti, J. *Gateway to the Quranic Sciences*. Turath Publishing,
       2017.

[17]   Hanson, Y. H. *Rihla Lecture Series 2018*. 5 July 2018.

[18] Hanson, Y. H. "The Creed of Imam Al-Tahawi." Zaytuna Institute, California, 2007.

[19] Addaraqutni, A. Sunan Ad-Daraqutni, Dar Ibn Hazm.

[20] Schimmel, A. *And Muhammad is His Messenger: The Veneration of the Prophet in Islamic Piety.* UNC Press Books, 2014.

[21] Al-Maliki, M. I. A. *Muhammad the Perfect Man.* Visions of Reality Books, 2012.

[22] Khan, F. *Rihla Lecture Series 2018.* 5 July 2018.

[23] SInternational. *The Quran.* Abul-Qasim Publishing House, 1997.

[24] Kumek, Y. J. *Practical Mysticism: Sufi Journeys of Heart and Mind.* Kendall Hunt Publishing Company, 2018.

[25] Vahide, S. *The Collection of Light.* ihlas nur publication, 2001.

[26] Tirmizi, M. *Jami At-Tirmizi.* Dar-us-Salam, 2007.

[27] Esposito, J. L. *What Everyone Needs to Know about Islam.* Oxford University Press, 2011.

[28] Griffith, S. *The Church in the Shadow of the Mosque: Christians and Muslims in the World of Islam (Jews, Chrsitians, and Muslims from the Ancient to the Modern World).* Princeton University Press, 2012.

[29] Ajibah, A. B. *The Book of Ascension to the Essential Truths of Sufism.* Fonts Vitae, 2011.

[30] Elsadda, H. "Discourses on Women's Biographies and Cultural Identity: Twentieth-Century Representations of the Life of 'A'isha Bint Abi Bakr." *Feminist Studies,* vol. 27, no. 1, 2001, pp. 37–64.

[31] Barlas, A. *"Believing Women" in Islam: Unreading Patriarchal Interpretations of the Quran.* University of Texas Press, 2003.

[32] Sultuan, S. N. *The Quran and Sayings of Prophet Muhammad.* skylight paths publishing, 2007.

[33] Rahman, F. *Islam and Modernity: Transformation of an Intellectual Tradition.* University of Chicago Press, 1984.

[34] Majah, I. *Sunan Ibn-i-Majah.* Kitab Bhavan, 2000.

[35] Sardar, Z. *The Touch of Midas: Science, Values, and Environment in Islam and the West.* Manchester University Press, 1984.

[36] Kumek, Y. J. *Perils of Translation: Text and Behavior "A Common Word Among Us" in the Quran [3:64].* Unpublished manuscript, 2017.

[37] Chesterman, A. *Memes of Translation.* John Benjamins Publishing Company, 1997, p. 93.

[38] Miroslow Volf, G. b. M. a. M. Y. *A Common Word*. Wm. B. Eerdmans Publishing Co., 2010.

[39] As-Suyuti, J. *Tafsir Al-Quran Al-Azim (Commentary on the Quran)*. Dar ul Fikr, 1998.

[40] Osman, S. "Iqra," 24 June 2002. http://www.iqra.net/names/ QuranNames.html. Accessed 2018.

[41] Seyyed Hossein Nasr, *The Study Quran: A New Translation and Commentary*. HarperCollins, 2015.

[42] Div. Yale, "Yale Center for Faith & Culture," 24 July 2008. http:// faith.yale.edu/common-word/2008-conference. Accessed 19 September 2016.

[43] Crone, P. "Jewish Christianity and the Quran." *Journal of Near Eastern Studies*, 2010, pp. 225–53.

[44] Yildirim, S. *Quran & Its Translation with Commentary*. Feza, 1998, p. 57.

[45] Munday, J. *The Routledge Companion to Translation Studies*. Routledge, 2009, p. 52.

[46] Amjad, F. A. "Problems and Strategies in English Translation of Quranic Divine Names." *International Journal of Linguistics*, 2013, pp. 128–42.

[47] Jones, F. R. "On Aboriginal Sufferance: A Process Model of Poetic Translating." *Target*, 1989, pp. 183–99.

[48] Macfarquhar, N. "New York Times," 12 October 2007. www. nytimes.com/2007/10/12/us/12muslims.html?&_r=0. Accessed 19 September 2016.

[49] BBC. "BBC News," 12 October 2007. [Online]. news.bbc.co.uk/2/ hi/europe/7038992.stm. Accessed 19 September 2016.

[50] Njeru, M. V. "Are Translators Traitors? A Philosophical Perspective of Loss and Gain in Translation." *Global Journal of Human-Social Science*, vol. 15, no. 8, 2015, pp. 2249–60.

[51] Toorawa, S. "Hapless Hapaxes and Luckless Rhymes: The Quran as Literature." *Religion & Literature*, vol. 41, 2009, pp. 221–27.

[52] Ekin, Y. Kur'an Tercüme Teknikleri (Tecniques of Translating the Quran), Işık Yayıncılık Ticaret, 2015.

[53] Mir, Mustansir. "The Quran as Literature." *Religion & Literature*, 1988: 49–64.

[54] Mir, Mustansir. "Dialogue in the Quran." *Religion and Literature*, 1992: 1–22.

[55] Abu-Zayd, Nasr. "The Dilemma of the Literary Approach to the Quran." *Journal of Comparative Poetics*, 2003: 8–47.

[56] P. Rietbroek, "Brill's simple Arabic transliteration system," *Brill*, 2010.

[57] Razi, M. *Mafatih al-Ghayb known as al-Tafsir al-Kabir*. Dar Ibya al-Kutub al-Bahiyya, 1172.

[58] Khan, W. *Quran: A Simple English Translation*. Goodword, 2013.

[59] As-Sabuni, A. *Rawai'u al-Bayan Tafsir ayat al-Ahkam Min al-Qur'an*. Beirut, 1983.

[60] Kasir, I. *Tafsir al-Quran al-Azim*. Dar al-Ilm, 1982.

[61] Speight, R. M. *Interreligious documents: Guidelines for Dialogue between Christians and Muslims*. Paulist Press, 1990.

[62] Cornell, V. J. e. a. *Do Jews, Christians, and Muslims Worship the Same God?* Abingdon Press, 2012.

[63] Arberry, A. *Interpretation of Koran*. Macmillan, 1955.

[64] Senapati, B. P. *Jesus the Kalimatullah: A Christian-Muslim Relation*. Cambridge Press, 2009.

[65] Gunton, C. E. *The Cambridge Companion to Christian Doctrine*. Cambridge University Press, 1997, pp. 78, 124, & 127.

[66] Malak, A. *Muslim Narratives and the Discourse of English*. SUNY Press, 2007.

[67] Demirci, M. *Tefsir Tarihi (History of Exegesis of Quran)*. ifav, 2010, pp. 34–38.

[68] U. P. Oxford, "Oxford Dictionaries," 2016. http://www.oxforddictionaries.com/us/definition/american_english/say. Accessed 2016.

[69] Anjum, Z. *Iqbal: The Life of a Poet, Philosopher and Politician*. Random House India, 2014.

[70] Sells, M. *Approaching the Quran: The Early Revelation*. White Cloud Press, 1999.

[71] Al-Marghinani, B. F. *Al-Hidayah: The Guidance*. Amal Press, 2006.

GLOSSARY

'Abd   worshipper, servant, or slave

Accountability   liability, especially in Islam and in Abrahamic traditions, everyone has a free will or agency in this world but accountability for their actions in the afterlife in front of Allah سبحانه وتعالى

Adab   good manners, especially in the relationship with Allah سبحانه وتعالى in Sufism

Adjective   attribute, a phrase describing a noun

Adonai   name of Allah سبحانه وتعالى in Judaism

Affair   relationship

Agency   acting as an agent or a carrier with free will

Alhamdulillah   a chanted divine phrase of appreciation of Allah سبحانه وتعالى

Alienating   isolating, separating, disconnecting

Alienating Images of Allah   understandings about Allah سبحانه وتعالى that disconnects person to establish a regular relationship with the Divine or to follow a religion

Allah   proper name of the One and Only Unique Creator, with other numerous names and attributes, translated in English as Allah سبحانه وتعالى.

Allude   explain, refer

Anger   uncontrolled and chaotic human spiritual state

Aphorism   sayings, proverbs in a culture, society, or belief

Appreciate   thank

Appreciative   with capital A, Allah سبحانه وتعالى

Arabic   language, especially the language of revelation of the Quran

Arrogance   feelings and actions of superiority

Ascension   rising, especially in Sufism, increase of spiritual states in relationship with Allah سبحانه وتعالى

Assert   claim

Astagfirullah   a divine phrase of asking forgiveness from Allah سبحانه وتعالى and cleaning the heart

Attribute   adjective, a phrase describing a noun, especially in Sufism

Attributes of Allah   divine phrases describing Allah سبحانه وتعالى

Authentic   original, genuine, true

Balance   modesty, especially in Sufism, following the middle way

Behavior   temporary nature of a person

Bismillah   a divine phrase of starting something with the blessing of Allah سبحانه وتعالى

Book of Chant   the Quran

Boost   increase

Bowing down   bending one's body, especially the act of respect by bending one's body, for Allah سبحانه وتعالى

Caution   carefulness, alertness, especially in Sufism, in spiritual manners not to be trapped by ego or self

Certainty   knowing without doubt, especially in Sufism, knowing and experiencing without doubt

Chanting   repeating, especially in Sufism, repeating the phrases with focus and experience

Chaos   disorder and confusion, especially in Sufism (spiritual) chaos being in negative states of anxiety, stress, and purposelessness

Charge   positive states of spirituality that makes the person happy, peaceful, and calm, filling oneself with divine knowledge and experience

Compassion   loving and caring

Confirming Book   the Quran

Confirming Scripture   the Quran

Conscience   internal instinct of distinguishing right or wrong

Consciousness   awareness

Constant   not changing, permanent, especially in practice, known as Reflective Attributes of Allah سبحانه وتعالى, where humans have an image but Allah سبحانه وتعالى has its source

Construction   formation of an abstract entity

Contract   squeeze

Convergence   similarity

Cosmology   knowledge about the origin and development of the universe

Covenant   agreement

Death   end of physical faculties of a person, especially physical versus spiritual death; the soul does not die but the body dies in understanding of physical death in Islam

Dedication   sincere constant effort

Deity   representation of the transcendent

Detox   discharge

Devout   pious, practicing

Dhikr   as one of the names of the Quran, or any type of chant to remember Allah سبحانه وتعالى

Discharge   negative states of spirituality that makes the person sad, stressed, and anxious, especially in Sufism, emptying oneself from all the temporal and worldly positive and negative attachments

Divine   transcendent

Doctrine   teaching

Dominance   control

Dream   visions when one is sleeping or awake

Ego   self, identifier of a person, especially in Sufism, raw and uneducated identifier and controller of a person

Elohim   name of Allah سبحانه وتعالى in Judaism

Embodiment, versus embody   making it part of one's character

Endeavor   engagement, activities

Epistemology   theory of knowledge

Ethical   moral

Ethnographic   based on observation

Etiquette   good manners and respect, especially in Sufism, respect in the relationship with Allah سبحانه وتعالى

Evil   anything that causes stress, sadness, or anxiety

Evil eye   the belief of unknown effects of the human eye across different cultures, traditions, and religions; especially in Sufism the evil eye effects due to extreme hatred, jealousy, or oppositely, evil eye effects due to extreme veneration and love of someone

Expand   enlarge

Experience   internalization of knowledge

Experience or experiential knowledge   all types of learning except from a book or a teacher, internalizing and personalizing the formal learning

Figurative   unclear, secondary and metaphorical

Free Will   free choice of a person in decision-making

Generous   with capital G, Allah سبحانه وتعالى

Genre   type

Genuine   sincere, original, authentic

Ghazali   philosopher, theologician, Sufi mystic, lived in twelfth century

Glorification   the mental, spiritual, and maybe verbal act of describing Allah سبحانه وتعالى in an admirable way

Groundless   fake

Habitual   habit of doing something constantly

HasbiyaAllah   a chant with a meaning of "Allah سبحانه وتعالى is sufficient for me"

Heaven   a place of all maximized pleasures of bodily and spiritual engagements while being with Allah سبحانه وتعالى

Hell   a place of punishment

Humbleness   behavior of modesty in viewing oneself, accepting the weakness in one's relationship with Allah سبحانه وتعالى and not being disrespectful and arrogant to Allah سبحانه وتعالى

Humility   character or trait of humbleness

Illa Allah   "except Allah" or "except Allah سبحانه وتعالى"

Images of Allah   understandings and experiences about Allah سبحانه وتعالى

Imitation   trying without real understanding

Infinite   Allah سبحانه وتعالى, the Unlimited

Informant   a person who participates in anthropological research

InshAllah   Allah سبحانه وتعالى willing, hopefully

Intention   planning ideas before the action

Intrinsic   internal

Islam   name of a religion that emphasizes believing in one Allah God سبحانه وتعالى and Jesus عليه السلام, Moses عليه السلام, and Muhammad صلى الله عليه وسلم to be the human prophets of the Creator

Jihad   struggle, especially spiritual struggle within oneself

Joseph   Prophet of Allah سبحانه وتعالى in Islam, Christianity, and Judaism

Journey   struggles of following guidelines of a mystical school

Khidr   mystical being who is sent by Allah سبحانه وتعالى at any time to help people in their problems; also believed to be the teacher of Moses in a mystical journey as mentioned in the Quran

Kitab   the Quran

Knowledge   theoretical understanding of something through education

La ilaha illa Allah   there is no Allah سبحانه وتعالى except Allah, a critical Divine phrase of chanting in Sufism implying a spiritual charge and discharge

Literal   clear and primary

Lord   Allah سبحانه وتعالى

Lucifer   Satan, mentioned in divine scriptures such as the Bible and the Quran

Majnun   crazy or, especially in Sufism, heretic

Mantra   a repetitive phrase or sound, especially used in Hinduism and Buddhism

Meditation   deep focus especially with reflection

Memorization   learning by heart

Mercy   compassion and forgiveness

Middle way   living a balanced life in spiritual and worldly engagements

Mimic   imitate

Mind   logic, reason, and rationality

Miracle   incidents against the law of physics and against all natural sciences

Mosque   temple of Muslims

Muhammad   Prophet Muhammad, the last and final Prophet and Messenger sent by God after Jesus

Musaddiq   the Quran

Mystic   a person who adopts the teachings of mysticism

Mysticism   the knowledge of the transcendent

Nafs   self in its raw form

Neat   tidy and in order

Negation   denial, emptying from the mind and heart the imperfect ideas and feelings about Allah سبحانه وتعالى

Neglectful   not giving the proper attention that is due

Notion   concept, idea

Odd   not even, unique, no equivalence

One   with capital denoting the one and only Creator

Oppression unjust action of the strong over the weak

PBUH Peace Be Upon Him (Any of the Prophets/Messengers such as Abraham, Jesus, Moses, Muhammad) abbreviated as PBUH.

PBUT Peace Be Upon Them (All The Prophets/Messengers such as Abraham, Jesus, Moses, Muhammad) abbreviated as PBUT

Permanent constant, not changing, not ending

Permanent non-ending

Phenomenon occurrence

Pious devout, practicing

Pollution making something dirty

Pronunciation correct sounds of letters in a language

Prophet Muhammad the last and final Prophet and Messenger sent by God after Jesus

Prostration, versus to prostrate the act of respect by putting one's face on the ground, humbling oneself for Allah سبحانه وتعالى by putting the face, the noble part of the body, on the ground

Qibla the direction where Muslims turn when they pray

Quran sacred text of Muslims

Rabbinic related to the Rabbis, the priests, and teachers of Judaism

Rasulullah ﷺ the word Rasulullah can be translated as "the Messenger or Prophet of Allah." Rasulullah in its usage is the Prophet Muhammad (peace and blessings be upon him). The Arabic writing ﷺ is read as "Sallalahu alayhi wa sallam" abbreviated as "saws" and is said when the name of the Prophet Muhammad is mentioned. This expression is practically and commonly translated as "peace and blessings be upon him". The expressions ﷺ or saws are expressions and phrases of blessings, peace and respect for the Prophet Muhammad عليه السلام when his name is mentioned. There are also expressions and phrases of blessings and peace used for the other Prophets of Allah such as Abraham, Moses, Jesus, and others عليه السلام.

Recitation, versus to recite reading, versus to read

Reliance dependence

Repetition   repeating

Reverence   respect

Reward   prize, payment, especially in worldly and afterlife rewards in Islam

Ritual   practices in a religion or mysticism that have spiritual and divine value for a person

Rububiyyah   True Understanding and Practice of Caretaking and Nourishing Attribute of Allah سبحانه وتعالى

Ruku   bowing down

Rumi   great Sufi mystic

Saint   the person who believed to be close to Allah سبحانه وتعالى

Sakina   peaceful and calm feelings

Salawat   names of the chants to remember teachers and their covenants with their students, especially the main teacher, the Rasulullah ﷺ and others, such as Abraham عليه السلام, Moses, and Jesus

Samad   the One who does not need anything, but everyone and everything needs Allah سبحانه وتعالى

Satan   the Devil, Lucifer, mentioned in divine scriptures such as in the Bible and the Quran

Scent   perfume, nice smell

Scholar   expert, the experts who practice what they teach (alim)

Scripture   sacred book or sacred text

Self   ego, identifier of a person, raw and uneducated identifier and controller of a person

Service   ethical action of doing good for others and society

Spiritual Journey   struggles of following guidelines of a mystical school

State   level, especially in Sufism, spiritual level

Struggle   efforts to achieve a goal

SubhanAllah   glorification of Allah سبحانه وتعالى, a divine phrase of chanting of spirituality implying a spiritual charge and discharge

SubhanAllahu wa bihamdihi   a divine phrase of glorification of Allah سبحانه وتعالى

SubhanAllahul Azeem   a divine phrase of glorification of Allah سبحانه وتعالى in the prostration posture

SubhanRabbiyalAzim   phrase of glorification for Allah سبحانه وتعالى in the bowing posture

Submission   natural acceptance of the uncontrolled and unseen

Sufi   follower of Sufism

Sufism   mystical path of Islam

Superstitious   fake

Surrender   involuntary state of acceptance of the uncontrolled and the unseen

SWT   Allah سبحانه وتعالى: The expression سبحانه وتعالى read as Subhānahu wa Tā'la also abbreviated as SWT and written as also Allah (SWT) is an expression of respect when the Name of Allah is mentioned. Among these expressions many English translations, one can be "Allah is One, Unique and Perfect with all the Divine Attributes and Names, far beyond human's negative and wrong constructions and imaginations. All Glory Belongs to Allah, the Most Exalted, the Most Respected, and the Most High.

Tahajjud   night prayer

Talismanic   unknown and indescribable effects of divine words and sounds

Taqwa   respect of Allah سبحانه وتعالى

Tawhid   true understanding and practice of Oneness and Uniquness of Allah سبحانه وتعالى

Temple   worship place

Temporal   transitory

Temptation   false ideas

The Curer   Allah سبحانه وتعالى

The Divine   Allah سبحانه وتعالى

The Forgiver a name of Allah سبحانه وتعالى in Islam

The Friend a name of Allah سبحانه وتعالى in Islam

The Helper a name of Allah سبحانه وتعالى in Islam

The Lover a name of Allah سبحانه وتعالى in Islam

The Peace Giver Allah سبحانه وتعالى

The Real Allah سبحانه وتعالى

The Real Maker Allah سبحانه وتعالى

The Reminder the Quran

The Source Allah سبحانه وتعالى

The Sustainer a name of Allah سبحانه وتعالى in Sufism

The Wise with capital W, Allah سبحانه وتعالى

Throne a figurative or metaphorical representation of dominion of Allah سبحانه وتعالى

Trait permanent character or nature

Tranquility peace and calmness

Transcendent beyond human limits

Transitory temporal

Transliteration writing the sounds of words or phrases in one language with an alphabet of another language

Ubudiyyah True Understanding and Practice of Worship of Allah سبحانه وتعالى

Uluhiyyah True Understanding and Practice of Divinity of Allah سبحانه وتعالى

Union being together, especially in this book, goal and joy of being always in the presence of Allah سبحانه وتعالى

Unseen anything five senses cannot testify in scientific methods

Weak not having a physical strength to perform an action, especially in Sufism, not having spiritual strength to perform any action

Worshipper a person who regularly follows and practices rituals, acts of prayers

ACKNOWLEDGMENTS

I would like to thank all my unnamed teachers, friends, and students for their input, ideas, suggestions, help, and support during and before the preparation of this book.

I would like to thank Professor David Banks, faculty of the Department of Anthropology, State University of New York (SUNY) at Buffalo, for meeting with me daily to go over the manuscript. I would like to thank Mufti Asim of Darul Uloom Al-Madania of Buffalo, Sheikh Ali of Hartford Seminary, Sheikh Tamer of Jami Masjid for all their valuable suggestions.

Lastly, I would like to thank all of my family members for their patience with me during the preparation of this book.

ABOUT THE AUTHOR

Dr. Yunus (Jonah) Kumek is currently teaching at Harvard Divinity School on Islam. He has been religious studies coordinator at State University of New York (SUNY) Buffalo State and teaching undergraduate and graduate courses in religious studies at SUNY at Buffalo State, Niagara University and Daemen College. Before becoming interested in religious studies, Dr. Kumek was doing his doctorate degree in physics at SUNY at Buffalo published academic papers in the areas of quantum physics, and medical physics. Then, he decided to engage with the world of social sciences through social anthropology, education, and cultural anthropology in his doctorate studies. He later spent a few years as a research associate in the anthropology department of the same university and published a book about different cultures and beliefs of international teachers in America. Recently, he completed a postdoctoral fellowship at Harvard Divinity school and published books on religious literacy through ethnography and practical mysticism: Sufi journeys of heart and mind. Dr. Kumek had classical training in Islamic sciences from the teachers of Egypt, India, Turkey, Yemen, Somalia, Morocco, and the United States. He stayed and studied in Egypt and Turkey. Dr. Kumek, who remains interested in physics—solves physics problems to relax—enjoys different languages, German, Spanish, Arabic, Hebrew, Urdu, and Turkish, especially in his research of scriptural analysis. Dr. Kumek takes great pleasure in classical poetry as well.

INDEX